# SAVEUR

# The New
# Comfort Food

*Camille Lebro, a home cook in Paris, preparing seven-hour leg of lamb. (For a recipe, see page 142.)*

# SAVEUR

# The New Comfort Food

## Home Cooking from Around the World

Edited by James Oseland

CHRONICLE BOOKS

SAN FRANCISCO

# Table of Contents

*A home cook in Oneida County, New York, frosts a spiced pumpkin cake for a community potluck supper.*

# Introduction

Last night I cooked the perfect meal. There was nothing new or unusual about it, just split pea soup and frisée salad, recipes I've known for years. But the crisp, bitter greens were studded with smoky bacon, and the yolk of a just-poached egg ran luxuriously over the top. The soup, made with leftovers from a ham I'd baked the day before, was warming and rich. Together with a hunk of crusty bread, these dishes made me incomparably happy.

Foods like these—comfort foods—we don't just eat, we hunger for. They are the chicken soup that's been simmering on the stove all afternoon, filling the house with tantalizing aromas. Or the macaroni and cheese, the version with béchamel and Gruyère, that your family and friends beg you to make. You eat them on the fly, standing up at market stalls: *shakshuka*, eggs poached in a spicy tomato stew, scooped from a curbside pot in Jerusalem; or crisp-fried spring rolls stuffed with pork and rice noodles, gobbled in a busy Bangkok market. They are restaurant classics: the crunchy fried chicken that a neighborhood joint is famous for, or the linguine tossed in white-wine sauce with mussels and shrimp at that Italian-American place we keep going back to. No matter where they're eaten, comfort foods are the ones we've known and loved forever; the ones we ate as kids and the ones we yearn for as adults. They're the foods that taste like home, wherever you happen to be when you eat them.

These are the dishes that we've always celebrated in the pages of SAVEUR magazine: soulful, honest, traditional fare that transcends trend and defines the way people eat all over the globe. Every cuisine has its canon of comfort, the foods that folks crave above all others and the ones they eat day in and day out. Those are the recipes you'll find in this book: for good, old American stick-to-your-ribs fare, like Texas chili, Rhode Island stuffed clams, chicken pot pie, and patty melts; and for international dishes like guacamole and French onion soup, whose comfort the world has claimed as its own. There are the great pastas of Italy, like fettuccine Alfredo—that irresistible tangle of pasta, butter, and cheese—and homemade tagliatelle egg noodles with slow-simmered, meaty *ragù bolognese*. There are the lusty one-pot meals, like *boeuf à la bourguignonne,* and oven-baked triumphs like potatoes gratin—dishes that French cooks affectionately call *cuisine grand-mère*, or grandma's cuisine. All told, this compendium represents some of the best traditional home cooking on the planet.

There's also something new about this collection of comfort foods. It reflects just how much the category has grown. If you're like me—I came of age in postwar California, raised by parents

*Hair and makeup artists, working at a fashion show at the Millennium Biltmore Hotel in Los Angeles, break for a lunch of burgers.*

*Shoppers at the Mercato Orientale, a busy market in the heart of Genoa, Italy.*

*Diners enjoy peel-and-eat boiled shrimp from the Gulf of Mexico.*

who loved to cook—you might have grown up on a far-reaching diet of foods like tamales, bagels and lox, Chinese spareribs, and, yes, meat loaf. But today, our comfort-food vocabulary is even broader. We have access to it all: fresh lemongrass, Israeli couscous, handmade corn tortillas, dried *baccalà*. We travel more. America's population continues to become more diverse. And we've learned volumes about the way the world eats.

At SAVEUR, we've always been interested in where these foods come from, and we've trekked to the places where they're produced. We've marveled at the producers' ingenuity: the gristmills that grind wheat into flour, the aging rooms where cheeses develop their flavors. We've come to understand the historical and cultural contexts that shape a cuisine's character: the trade routes, the agricultural traditions, the ways people obtain their food. We've learned to use cooking tools like seasoned woks for making Chinese stir-fries and clay *tagines* for Moroccan stews, and we've embraced techniques for everything from extracting the flavor from lemongrass to evenly slicing carrots.

Most of all, we've come to know and admire the people who acquainted us with these dishes. Some of them are chefs, to be sure, but most are people making a living serving great food—like José and Gloria Fonseca of Los Angeles's La Abeja café, whose huevos rancheros introduced me to the pleasures of Mexican breakfast; and the Mississippi Delta line cook Brandon Hughes, who deep-fries catfish like nobody's business. They're home cooks preparing meals for family and friends: people like SAVEUR contributor Alia Yunis, who gave us her Palestinian-Lebanese mother's exemplary recipe for hummus; Aggeliki Bakali, from the Greek village of Pertouli, who taught us how to make *hortopita*, a savory pie of wild greens wrapped in homemade phyllo dough; and even my dad, Larry, whose method for marinating and grilling flank steak yields a charred, salty crust and a perfectly pink center.

This book is a tribute to those great cooks and to all the valuable lessons we've learned from them over the years. In the sidebars and notes that run alongside the recipes, our editors and contributors share their stories, as well as kitchen wisdom and ingredient information that inspire and empower us as cooks. The dishes these people make is food for the body and soul. We can't help but give ourselves over to it. That's the beautiful thing about comfort food: no matter where it comes from, it awakens our senses and lifts our spirits. It comforts us again and again.

—*JAMES OSELAND*

# Snacks, Starters, and Salads

Every corner of the globe has its favorites: Thai spring rolls, Argentine empanadas, Italian crostini. From the Mediterranean and the Middle East, where snacking on small plates is a way of life, we get hummus drizzled with aromatic olive oil, vegetable-filled savory pies, and grilled bread topped with peak-of-season ingredients like wild mushrooms or sweet, juicy tomatoes. If you ask us, there's no more convivial way to eat than laying out a table full of these flavorful starters and inviting everyone to dive in.

*A variety of mezedes, or small plates, at Tsinari, an ouzeri in the city of Thessaloniki, in northern Greece.*

# The Ultimate Grilled Cheese Sandwich

The French cows' milk cheese Comté is one of the best melting cheeses we know of. The key to bringing out its mildly sharp, herbaceous flavors is to cook it very slowly in a generous amount of butter over moderate heat, allowing it to relax into a luscious melt—in this case between two thick slices of sourdough bread.

4   tbsp. unsalted butter, softened
4   ½-inch-thick slices sourdough bread
8   oz. Comté cheese, grated

*Serves 2*

**1.** Spread the butter evenly on both sides of each slice of bread. Put half the cheese on one slice and half on another. Top each with a remaining bread slice.

**2.** Heat a 12-inch cast-iron skillet over medium-low heat. Add the sandwiches to the skillet and cook, flipping once with a metal spatula, until golden brown and crusty on both sides, 9–10 minutes each side. Transfer the sandwiches to a cutting board and slice in half with a knife.

**COOKING NOTE** *While Comté makes the ultimate grilled cheese sandwich, other semifirm cheeses—including Jarlsberg, fontina, and Gruyère—melt beautifully, too.*

## The Real Thing

As much as I loved grilled American cheese sandwiches as a kid, it wasn't until a few years ago that I discovered how transcendent this classic comfort food can taste when it's made with truly great cheese. That epiphany came after a visit to the Jura mountains, along the French-Swiss border. There, I was seduced by Comté, a semifirm cheese born of the distinctive milk of local Montbéliarde cows, whose diet

includes wild orchids, daisies, dandelions, and more than 400 other plant varieties that grow on the green hillsides of the Franche-Comté region. Produced in the *fruitières,* or cooperative dairies, that have dotted this landscape for centuries, the wheels of cheese are aged on spruce boards for a few weeks before being entrusted to an *affineur,* or cellar master, who oversees its further maturation. Unlike many AOC cheeses (meaning those from specially designated cheese-making regions), Comté is made with an emphasis not on uniformity but on individuality. A young cheese that's just a few months old may taste and smell like butter, an older one that's been aged for a year or more, like fruit and spices. Over time, the cheese develops hints of chocolate, spice, nutmeg, apricot, hazelnut, and caramel, flavors that become even more prominent, I discovered, once the cheese has melted. It's no wonder that Comté is such a celebrated cooking cheese, used in both France and the United States for everything from fondues to soufflés to gratins to my personal favorite, great grilled cheese sandwiches.
—*Cara de Silva*

# Frisée Salad with Poached Eggs and Bacon

*Frisée aux Lardons*

This classic French bistro salad gets its savor and crunch from a liberal scattering of thick bacon slivers, which the French call *lardons*. SAVEUR contributor Eugenia Bone (pictured below) makes it with her own home-cured bacon, but any store-bought unsmoked slab bacon will work well. For tips on poaching eggs, see "Perfect Poaching" on page 64.

5   ½-inch-thick slices unsmoked slab bacon, sliced crosswise into ½-inch-wide strips
2   cups distilled white vinegar
     Kosher salt, to taste
4   large eggs
1   tbsp. minced shallots
1   tbsp. fresh lemon juice
2   tsp. Dijon mustard
2   tbsp. extra-virgin olive oil
     Freshly ground black pepper, to taste
½   lb. frisée greens, torn into medium-size pieces

*Serves 4*

**1.** Combine bacon and 1 cup water in a 12-inch skillet over medium-high heat. Cook, stirring, until water evaporates and bacon crisps, 30–40 minutes. Using a slotted spoon, transfer bacon to a plate. Reserve fat in skillet.

**2.** Prepare eggs for poaching: Bring 16 cups of water to a boil in a tall 6-qt. saucepan over high heat. Add the vinegar and 2 tsp. salt, lower heat to medium, and bring to a simmer. Crack each egg into its own ramekin and set aside. (Don't cook the eggs yet.)

**3.** In a medium bowl, whisk together shallots, lemon juice, mustard, and 3 tbsp. reserved bacon fat. While whisking, slowly drizzle in the olive oil to make a smooth vinaigrette. Season with salt and pepper. In a large bowl, toss frisée with vinaigrette. Divide frisée and bacon between 4 plates.

**4.** Swirl the simmering vinegar water with a spoon to create a whirlpool. Carefully slide each egg into the water and poach until just firm, 2–3 minutes. Using a slotted spoon, transfer the eggs to paper towels to drain, then top salads with 1 egg apiece. Season salads with salt and pepper. Serve immediately.

# Spring Rolls with Chile–Garlic Sauce

*Boh Biah Tote*

Crunchy fried spring rolls like these, stuffed with pork, mushrooms, and rice noodles and served with a sweet and spicy dipping sauce, are a popular midday snack in Thailand. Be sure to keep the reserved spring roll wrappers covered with a damp towel while you're working, to prevent them from drying out.

**FOR THE CHILE–GARLIC SAUCE:**

| | |
|---|---|
| 1 | cup sugar |
| ½ | cup distilled white vinegar |
| 2 | tbsp. minced garlic |
| 2 | tsp. kosher salt |
| 1 | tsp. cayenne pepper |

**FOR THE SPRING ROLLS:**

| | |
|---|---|
| 3 | dried mushrooms, such as cloud ear, porcini, or shiitake |
| 2 | oz. rice vermicelli noodles |
| ¼ | lb. ground pork |
| ¼ | lb. medium shrimp, peeled, deveined, and minced |
| 2 | tbsp. fish sauce |
| 2 | tbsp. minced shallots |
| ½ | tsp. freshly ground white pepper |
| ½ | tsp. sugar |
| 1 | clove garlic, minced Kosher salt, to taste |
| 7 | 6 inch square spring roll wrappers, quartered into small squares |
| 1 | egg, lightly beaten Peanut oil, for frying |

*Makes 28 rolls*

**1.** Make the chile–garlic sauce: In a 2-qt. saucepan, bring the sugar, vinegar, garlic, salt, and ½ cup water to a boil over medium heat. Stir to dissolve the sugar and reduce the heat to low. Simmer until the liquid is thick and syrupy, about 20 minutes. Remove the pan from the heat, stir in the cayenne, and transfer to a serving bowl. Chill until ready to use.

**2.** Make the spring rolls: Put the mushrooms into a small bowl, cover with hot water, and let soak until soft, about 20 minutes. Meanwhile, put the noodles into a large bowl and cover with hot water; let soak until soft, about 6 minutes. Drain and roughly chop the noodles; set aside. Drain the mushrooms and finely chop them. In a large bowl, combine the noodles and mushrooms along with the pork, shrimp, fish sauce, shallots, white pepper, sugar, and garlic. Mix the filling together and season lightly with salt.

**3.** Working with 1 small square of spring roll wrapper at a time, put the wrapper on a work surface so that one corner faces you. Ⓐ Put 1 scant tbsp. of filling in the center

of the wrapper, and brush the far edge of the wrapper with a little of the beaten egg. Ⓑ Fold the near corner up over the filling to make a cylinder, and cinch the cylinder to make sure the filling is tightly wrapped. Ⓒ Fold the sides of the wrapper into the center of the cylinder. Ⓓ Roll the cylinder toward the far corner until the spring roll is sealed. Transfer the spring roll, seam side down, to a plate. Repeat with the remaining filling and wrappers; set aside.

**4.** Pour oil to a depth of 2 inches into a 6-qt. heavy-bottomed pot over medium-high heat. Heat until a deep-fry thermometer reads 350°F. Working in batches, fry the spring rolls, turning, until golden, about 3 minutes. Transfer to a paper towel–lined plate. Serve the spring rolls with the chile–garlic sauce.

## Know Your Artichokes

Scores of different artichoke cultivars are grown around the world. Pictured on facing page and described below are nine of our favorites that are commercially available in the United States.

① Developed in the mid-1980s by a California grower, the **big heart** is aptly named. It is endowed with a large, fleshy base and weighs in at over a pound. Excellent for stuffing.

② The classic **green globe**, sometimes called just the globe, has a buttery-tasting heart and bottom and an ample amount of meat at the base of the leaves. This artichoke, which ranges in size from three to five inches in diameter, was originally brought to California from Italy.

③ The two-inch-wide **fiesole** artichoke has a fruity flavor and a deep wine color that does not fade with cooking. Bred from the *violetta de provence*, a purple variety native to southern France, the *fiesole* has a comparatively tender stalk that can be quickly steamed and eaten.

④ The oblong **siena**, about four inches in diameter and born of a breeding program in central Italy, has a small choke and a wine-red color. Slow to mature and still grown in relatively small quantities, this petite artichoke usually weighs less than a pound and has a heart tender enough to be eaten raw.

⑤ The four-inch-wide **lyon** is classically shaped and has a maroon tint to its leaves. A versatile, all-purpose artichoke.

⑥ Light red and roughly one inch in diameter when fully grown, the purple **baby anzio** is a relative of the *romanesco* artichoke of the Lazio region of Italy. Like many baby artichokes, baby *anzios* can be eaten whole.

⑦ The dense and rotund **omaha** is less bitter than many artichoke varieties. Great for stuffing.

⑧ The **chianti**, a wide green artichoke with a touch of maroon on the leaves, is tender and a good choice for boiling.

⑨ The vividly colored **king** has green spots on the tips of its leaves. Relatively small, it has a soft heart that makes this a great choice for steaming or grilling.

# Italian-Style Stuffed Artichokes

*Carciofi Stufati*

Artichokes, in an abundance of colors and sizes, are a springtime fixture in markets across Italy, and cooks there do wonderful things with them. This classic antipasto, in which full-size globe artichokes are stuffed with a mixture of garlic, Pecorino Romano, and bread crumbs and baked until tender, is one of our all-time favorites.

| | |
|---|---|
| 4 | large artichokes |
| 1 | lemon, halved |
| 1¾ | cups dried bread crumbs |
| 1 | cup freshly grated Pecorino Romano |
| ⅓ | cup chopped flat-leaf parsley |
| 2 | tsp. kosher salt |
| 1 | tsp. freshly ground black pepper |
| 8 | cloves garlic, minced |
| 5 | tbsp. extra-virgin olive oil |

*Serves 4*

**1.** Using a serrated knife, cut off the artichoke stems to create a flat bottom. Cut the top third off each artichoke, pull off the tough outermost leaves, and trim the sharp tips of the leaves with kitchen shears. Rub the cut parts with the lemon halves. Open the artichoke leaves with your thumbs to make room for the stuffing; set aside.

**2.** Heat the oven to 425°F. In a large bowl, combine the bread crumbs, ¾ cup cheese, parsley, salt, pepper, and garlic. Working with 1 artichoke at a time over a bowl, sprinkle one-quarter of the bread crumb mixture over the artichoke and work it in between the leaves. Transfer the stuffed artichoke to a shallow baking dish and repeat with the remaining artichokes.

**3.** Drizzle each artichoke with 1 tbsp. oil. Pour boiling water to a depth of 1 inch into the baking dish. Rub 1 tbsp. olive oil on a sheet of aluminum foil, cover the artichokes with the foil (oiled side down), and secure the foil tightly around the dish with kitchen twine. Bake until a knife easily slides into the base of an artichoke, about 45 minutes. Remove the foil, sprinkle the artichokes with the remaining cheese, and heat the oven to broil. Broil until the tops of the artichokes are golden brown, about 3 minutes.

# Tapas-Style Meatballs

*Albóndigas en Salsa*

Succulent miniature meatballs, simmered in a sauce of olive oil, beef stock, and white wine, can be had throughout Spain, from the tapas bars of Madrid to the kitchens of home cooks like Carmen Barrio Perez (pictured at left), who lives in the small Catalan city of Sils. The meatballs are typically skewered with toothpicks and served in earthenware dishes called *cazuelas*.

**FOR THE MEATBALLS:**

- 1½ lbs. coarsely ground beef
- 1½ lbs. coarsely ground pork
- ½ cup fresh white bread crumbs
- ¼ cup minced flat-leaf parsley
- 4 eggs, lightly beaten
- 4 cloves garlic, minced
  Kosher salt and freshly ground black pepper, to taste
- 1 cup flour
- 1 cup extra-virgin olive oil, preferably Spanish

**FOR THE SAUCE:**

- 4 cloves garlic, minced
- 1 large yellow onion, chopped
- 1 large leek, white part only, chopped
- 1 dried bay leaf
- 2 tbsp. flour
- 2½ cups beef or veal stock
- 1½ cups white wine

*Serves 4–6*

**1.** Make the meatballs: Mix together the beef, pork, bread crumbs, parsley, eggs, garlic, and salt and pepper in a large bowl. Refrigerate for about 1 hour to chill.

**2.** Put the flour into a shallow bowl. Moisten your hands with water and divide the meat mixture into 20 even portions; roll portions into meatballs. Roll each meatball in flour, shake off the excess, and transfer to a baking sheet.

**3.** Heat ½ cup olive oil in a large skillet over medium-high heat. Brown half the meatballs in the skillet, 10–12 minutes; transfer to a plate. Wipe out the skillet and repeat with the remaining oil and meatballs, leaving the oil and caramelized bits in the skillet.

**4.** Make the sauce: Heat the skillet (with the reserved oil) over medium-low heat. Add the garlic, onions, leeks, and bay leaf and cook, stirring occasionally, until soft, 12–15 minutes. Add the flour and cook, stirring, for 2 minutes. Whisk in the stock and wine, raise the heat to medium-high, and bring to a boil while whisking constantly. Reduce the heat to medium-low and simmer until thickened, 12–14 minutes. Let cool and discard the bay leaf.

**5.** Purée the sauce in a blender in batches. Return the sauce to the skillet along with the meatballs and bring to a boil over medium-high heat. Reduce the heat to medium-low and simmer until the sauce is thickened and the meatballs are cooked through, 16–18 minutes. Season with salt and pepper. Divide between 6-inch or 7-inch *cazuelas* (earthenware dishes) or bowls to serve.

Fried foods like latkes
have long been favored
during the eight days
of Hanukkah because
oil is considered
symbolic of the mir-
acle that is central
to the holiday, which
commemorates the
Jews' victory over
the Syrian-Greeks
in 164 B.C. and the
rededication of the
Temple in Jerusalem.
(According to Jewish
scripture, a single
day's worth of oil kept
the temple's sacred
lamp lit for eight days.)
Every latke lover has
strong opinions about
the best way to pre-
pare the dish. Some
argue for using a food
processor to grate the
potatoes; others insist
on hand-grating them.
Most agree that this
rich dish calls for a
cool condiment—
typically, sour cream
or applesauce—and
many cooks enhance
the classic potato ver-
sion by adding grated
celery root, apple, zuc-
chini, beets, or acorn
squash to the mix.
Others remain purists,
making latkes with
reasonably starchy
potatoes like russet
or Yukon Gold and
adding matzo meal or
bread crumbs, as well
as egg, to help hold the
pancakes together.
Whatever ingredients
you use, slowly fry-
ing latkes in oil gives
them their distinctive
crisp-on-the-outside,
tender-on-the-inside
character. —*Joan
Nathan*

# Golden Potato Latkes

Potato pancakes, bolstered with grated onion and fried until crisp and lightly browned, have held a central place at Jewish holiday tables since the mid-nineteenth century, a time when the potato was becoming a widespread crop in Eastern Europe. They remain a beloved standby at Hanukkah, in particular. Sour cream or apple-sauce, both popular accompaniments, balance the latkes' rich flavor.

| | |
|---|---|
| 1 | medium yellow onion |
| 3 | large Yukon Gold potatoes (about 2 ½ lbs.), peeled |
| | Kosher salt, to taste |
| 6 | tbsp. minced fresh chives |
| 3 | tbsp. plain matzo meal |
| 2 | large eggs, lightly beaten |
| | Freshly ground white pepper, to taste |
| | Canola oil, for frying |
| | Sour cream or applesauce, for serving |

*Serves 6*

**1.** Working over a bowl, grate some of the onion, followed by some of the potatoes, on the large-hole side of a box grater. Repeat until all the vegetables are shredded.

**2.** Sprinkle the potato mixture with salt and transfer to a sieve set over a bowl. Squeeze out as much liquid as possible from the mixture, allowing it to collect in the bottom of the bowl. Transfer the potato mixture to another bowl and cover the surface with plastic wrap; set aside. Set the reserved potato liquid aside to let the milky white starch settle. Pour off the liquid from the starch. Transfer the starch to the potato mixture along with the chives, matzo meal, eggs, and pepper. Gently mix.

**3.** Pour oil into a skillet to a depth of ¼ inch and heat over medium-high heat. Working in small batches, form the potato mixture into balls, using about ¼ cup of the mixture for each, and place them in the oil. Flatten each ball gently with a spatula to form 3-inch to 4-inch pancakes. Fry, turning once, until golden brown, crisp, and cooked through, about 8 minutes. Transfer the latkes to a paper towel–lined plate to drain. Serve the latkes warm with sour cream or applesauce.

# Guacamole

Dozens of styles of this classic avocado dip can be found across Mexico, from elegantly smooth versions to chunky, rustic ones like this, in which diced jalapeños and fresh cilantro add bright notes to the creamy avocado. It comes from the New York City restaurant Rosa Mexicano, which in the 1980s popularized the trend of having servers make guacamole tableside in a *molcajete*, or mortar.

| | |
|---|---|
| 3 | tbsp. minced fresh cilantro leaves |
| 2 | tbsp. minced white onion |
| 2 | tsp. minced jalapeño |
| 1 | tsp. kosher salt, plus more to taste |
| 3 | medium-ripe Hass avocados (about 1½ lbs.) |
| 3 | tbsp. chopped, seeded tomato |
| | Tortilla chips, for serving |

*Serves 4*

**1.** In a mortar, using a pestle, pulverize 1 tbsp. cilantro, 1 tbsp. onions, jalapeño, and 1 tsp. salt to a paste. (Alternatively, on a cutting board, finely chop and scrape the ingredients into a paste and transfer to a bowl.) Set the onion mixture aside.

**2.** Cut the avocados in half lengthwise. Twist the halves to separate them, and remove the pits with the tip of the knife. Place an avocado half, cut side up, in your palm and make 3 or 4 evenly spaced lengthwise cuts through its flesh down to the skin, without cutting through the skin. Make 4 crosswise cuts in the same fashion.

**3.** Scoop the diced avocado flesh into the mortar or bowl. Repeat with the remaining avocados. Gently fold the avocado pieces into the onion paste, keeping the avocado pieces fairly intact.

**4.** Add the remaining cilantro and onions, along with the tomatoes. Fold together all the ingredients and season with salt. Serve immediately, directly from the mortar (or bowl), with the tortilla chips.

## Love Fruit

Today, they're almost as common as apples, but avocados have not always been an easy sell. In fact, it took more than 50 years of creative marketing to get Americans to embrace them. Growers—and, more important, the advertisers they hired—had to convince consumers that these exotic fruits were fashionable. How did they do it? Like any successful marketer, they hawked status, patriotism, and sex. Taking their lead from the success of the California orange industry, the avocado growers of California formed their own cooperative, in 1924. Initially, Calavo, as the organization came to be called, positioned the avocado as a substitute for meat. By the late 1920s and the 1930s, however, dieting was on the rise and salads were chic. So, Calavo began to attach new catchphrases to its product—"the aristocrat of salad fruits" was a favorite—in advertisements placed in magazines like *The New Yorker* and *Vogue*. In 1943, *California Farmer*, a trade magazine, ran an ad proclaiming that people with victory gardens (which were patriotically cultivated to provide food for civilians and troops) make their salads more delightful with avocados, which it called "grenades of glamour." Capitalizing on a vogue for things tropical in the 1950s, Calavo also encouraged consumers to associate the avocado with exotically themed party dishes that could be served at suburban luaus. Such strategies contributed considerably to America's love affair with guacamole. By the 1970s, Calavo's marketers had recognized the need to respond to a rapidly liberalizing society and media culture, and began fashioning a sexy image for the once humble avocado; one ad, in *McCall's* magazine, called the fruit the "love food from California." A California Avocado Commission print and billboard campaign from 1983 said it all: it pictured the movie star Angie Dickinson beside the words "Would this body lie to you?" Avocado sales reached an all-time high. —*Jeffrey Charles*

# Spicy Beef Empanadas

*Empanadas de Carne*

These fried pies are a ubiquitous snack in Argentina, and given the vast cattle ranches that fan out over the landscape there, beef is what you most often find inside. The ground beef in these empanadas gets a spicy kick from red chile flakes; chopped green olives add savory flavor. We based this recipe on one that appears in *Seven Fires: Grilling the Argentine Way* by Francis Mallmann.

| | |
|---|---|
| 4 | tbsp. lard or vegetable shortening |
| 1½ | tbsp. kosher salt, plus more, to taste |
| 6 | cups flour, plus more for dusting |
| 6 | tbsp. unsalted butter |
| 1 | lb. ground beef |
| 3 | medium yellow onions, quartered lengthwise, thinly sliced crosswise |
| 1 | tbsp. crushed red chile flakes |
| 1 | tbsp. ground cumin |
| 1 | tbsp. sweet Spanish smoked paprika |
| 4 | scallions, white and green parts kept separate, both minced |
| ¼ | cup fresh oregano leaves, minced |
| 2 | tbsp. extra-virgin olive oil Freshly ground black pepper, to taste |
| ½ | cup pitted green olives, minced |
| 2 | hard-boiled eggs, minced Canola oil, for frying |

*Serves 12*

**1.** Bring 3 tbsp. of the lard, 1½ tbsp. salt, and 2 cups water to a boil in a 1-qt. saucepan over high heat; pour into a large bowl and let cool to room temperature. Add the flour and mix until a dough forms. Transfer the dough to a lightly floured work surface and knead until smooth, 6–8 minutes. Halve the dough and flatten each half into a disk; wrap each disk in plastic and refrigerate for 1 hour.

**2.** Meanwhile, heat 4 tbsp. butter in a 12-inch skillet over medium-high heat. Add the beef and cook, stirring occasionally, until browned, about 15 minutes. Transfer the beef to a large bowl and set aside to cool. Return the skillet to the heat and add the remaining lard and butter. Add the onions and cook, stirring often, until soft, 10–12 minutes. Add the chile flakes, cumin, paprika, and the white parts of the scallions and cook, stirring often, for about 2 minutes. Remove from the heat and stir in the scallion greens, oregano, and olive oil; season with salt and pepper. Transfer the mixture to the bowl with the beef and stir to combine; set aside.

**3.** To form the empanadas, cut each dough disk in half and, working with one half at a time, roll the dough to a ⅛-inch thickness. Using a 5-inch round cookie cutter, cut out circles and transfer to a parchment paper–lined baking sheet. Repeat with the remaining dough, rerolling as needed to make 24 circles total. Working with one dough circle at a time, place 1 heaping tbsp. of the beef mixture in the middle and top it with a pinch of olives and egg. Lightly moisten the edge of the circle with water and fold the dough circle in half to form a turnover; pinch or crimp the dough to seal. Place on a baking sheet and repeat with the remaining dough circles, beef mixture, olives, and egg. Chill until ready to use.

**4.** Pour canola oil to a depth of 3 inches into a 6-qt. Dutch oven and heat over medium-high heat until a deep-fry thermometer reads 375°F. Working in batches, fry the empanadas, turning occasionally, until golden brown and crisp, 3–4 minutes. Transfer to a paper towel–lined plate to drain, and repeat with the remaining empanadas. Serve hot.

# Wild-Greens Pie

*Hortopita*

In many parts of Greece, harvesting wild herbs and greens and baking them into savory pies is an unbroken tradition dating back centuries. Aggeliki Bakali (pictured at left), a home cook in the central Greek village of Pertouli, makes this pie of greens, herbs, and feta from a family recipe that also calls for her to make her own phyllo dough, which she rolls into large circles to fit a 12-inch round cake pan. We found that store-bought country-style phyllo works just as well to make the pie in a 9 x 13-inch rectangular baking dish.

| | |
|---|---|
| 1 | cup plus 1 tbsp. extra-virgin olive oil |
| 16 | scallions, minced |
| 6 | cloves garlic, minced |
| 1¾ | lbs. Swiss chard (about 2 bunches), chopped |
| 1 | cup each minced fresh dill, mint, and parsley |
| | Kosher salt and freshly ground black pepper, to taste |
| 12 | oz. feta, crumbled |
| 1 | 16-oz. package frozen country-style phyllo dough, thawed |

*Serves 6–8*

1. Heat ½ cup oil in a pot over medium-high heat. Add scallions and garlic and cook, stirring, until soft, 3–4 minutes. Add chard and herbs and cook, stirring often, until tender, 12–15 minutes. Remove from the heat and season with salt and pepper. Let cool to room temperature and stir in feta; set aside.

2. Grease a 9 x 13-inch baking dish with 2 tbsp. oil. Cut 2 phyllo sheets into 11 x 15-inch sheets; layer them in the baking dish Ⓐ, brushing each with 2 tbsp. oil. Spread a third of the greens in pan on top of the phyllo.

3. Heat the oven to 400°F. Cut 4 phyllo sheets into 9 x 13-inch rectangles, and transfer to baking sheets. Bake each until golden, 4–6 minutes, and then set aside to cool. Place 2 baked phyllo sheets on top of greens and cover with half the remaining greens. Top with remaining 2 baked sheets and the remaining greens Ⓑ.

4. Cut 2 phyllo sheets into 9 x 13-inch rectangles. Cover greens with 1 sheet, and brush with 2 tbsp. oil; top with remaining phyllo and fold phyllo dough from the bottom layer hanging over edges onto top of pie. Brush top and edges with 1 tbsp. oil Ⓒ and score phyllo to vent. Bake for 20 minutes, reduce heat to 350°F, and bake until golden brown, 18–20 minutes. Let cool slightly and then cut into squares to serve Ⓓ.

One of the joys of living in Tuscany is that locals love a good party, which explains why many towns frequently hold communal meals and *sagre*—outdoor festivals that celebrate the harvest of a cherished local food. Such gatherings are a testament to Tuscans' abiding attachment to the seasonal rituals that are the foundation of rural life here. In Buggiano (pictured below), where I live, we have several alfresco feasts each year, but our summertime *cena* (the name simply means

dinner) is the most special because all of the food is prepared by local home cooks. The dinner, which is held in our main piazza, is a lavish potluck: there are platters of antipasti, including crostini topped with seasonal ingredients, and herbed tomato tarts (page 37). There are pastas, and a main dish of roast pork, fragrant with garlic and herbs. And for dessert: a spread of pastries, followed by glasses of locally made *limoncello*, and dancing that goes on late into the night. —*Beth Elon*

# Mushroom and Herb Crostini

*Crostini con Funghi*

Simple, satisfying crostini like these are among the many dishes prepared by SAVEUR contributor Beth Elon and her neighbors for a feast held each summer in their Tuscan town of Buggiano. We like the earthy flavor of cremini mushrooms in this classic antipasto, but you can use any variety of mushroom you like.

8   oz. mixed mushrooms, such as cremini, oyster, and button, stemmed and thinly sliced
7   tbsp. extra-virgin olive oil
3   tbsp. minced flat-leaf parsley
1   tbsp. fresh lemon juice
1   clove garlic, minced
    Kosher salt and freshly ground black pepper, to taste
8   slices country-style Italian bread, such as ciabatta
    Small wedge of Parmigiano-Reggiano

*Serves 4*

**1.** Heat the oven to 475°F. Toss together the mushrooms, 4 tbsp. oil, parsley, lemon juice, and garlic in a medium bowl. Season with salt and pepper and let sit at room temperature until the mushrooms have softened, about 20 minutes.

**2.** Put the bread slices on a baking sheet and brush with the remaining oil. Bake bread slices until golden brown, about 10 minutes. Let cool slightly, then spoon the mushroom mixture over the bread. Using a peeler, thinly slice strips of Parmigiano to garnish the crostini.

**COOKING NOTE** *The best way to clean mushrooms—rinse or soak in water, or wipe each mushroom with a damp cloth to avoid its taking in water—has long been a subject of debate. It took scientific proof to satisfy us once and for all. In an experiment described in the book* The Curious Cook, *author Harold McGee demonstrated that after soaking for five minutes, a button mushroom absorbs only one-sixteenth of a teaspoon of water. A speedy rinse, McGee concludes, results in virtually no water retention. The myth of the soggy mushroom, it turns out, just doesn't hold water.*

# Herbed Tomato Tart

Cookbook author Beth Elon, who lives in Buggiano, Italy, provided this recipe for a Tuscan-style cherry tomato tart. She prepared it for her village's annual outdoor summer feast (pictured at left; also see "Alfresco Feast," page 34), and it would serve just as well for any barbecue, picnic, or other outdoor meal.

2   9 x 11-inch sheets frozen puff pastry, thawed and chilled
½   cup freshly grated Parmigiano-Reggiano
4   tbsp. extra-virgin olive oil
12   anchovy filets in oil, drained and finely chopped
3   lbs. cherry or grape tomatoes
    Kosher salt and freshly ground black pepper, to taste
¼   cup minced flat-leaf parsley
2   tbsp. minced fresh chives
2   tbsp. minced fresh oregano
    Freshly grated nutmeg, to taste

*Serves 12–16*

**1.** Heat the oven to 375°F. Fit the pastry sheets side by side in a parchment paper–lined 13 x 17¾-inch rimmed baking pan, pressing the pastry against the bottom and sides. Press together the center where the two sheets overlap to make an even seam; trim the pastry hanging over the sides of the pan. Prick the bottom of the pastry with a fork. Line the bottom and sides of the pastry with parchment paper and fill with dried beans or pie weights. Bake until the edges of the tart are golden, about 25 minutes. Remove the beans and parchment paper, sprinkle Parmigiano-Reggiano over the tart shell, and bake until the cheese is melted and the tart shell is golden all over, 15–20 minutes. Transfer to a rack and let cool.

**2.** Heat the oven to broil and arrange a rack 4 inches from the heating element. In a large bowl, mix together the olive oil and anchovies; add the tomatoes and season with salt and pepper. Toss to coat. Transfer the tomato mixture to another rimmed baking pan and broil, shaking the pan once or twice, until the tomatoes blister, about 12 minutes. Remove the tomatoes from the oven and let them cool slightly. Use a slotted spoon to transfer the tomato mixture to the prepared tart shell and distribute the tomatoes evenly over the shell.

**3.** Lower the oven heat to 425°F. In a bowl, combine the parsley, chives, oregano, and nutmeg. Sprinkle the herb mixture evenly over the tomatoes. Return the tart to the oven and bake until hot, about 15 minutes. Let the tart cool slightly before serving, or serve at room temperature.

## Family Recipe

When my brother married a Polish-American girl named Rachael, my Palestinian-Lebanese mother held her breath. When they named their son after a baseball hero rather than my brother, she held her tongue. But when Rachael proudly served "black bean hummus" at a family party, my mother let it all out. "Hummus with black beans?" she said. "Why do Americans have to mix everything up until you can't even tell what is what? Hummus is just hummus!" That made me wonder what truly makes hummus hummus, so I polled my Arab-American friends and received passionate responses as to what genuine hummus was and was

not. Overwhelmingly, the responses were in favor of the traditional combination of ingredients—chickpeas, tahini, lemon juice, and garlic. In an act of Middle Eastern diplomacy, Rachael asked my mother how to make hummus the

"real way." My mom quickly listed the ingredients, giving no measurements or proportions. Always an advocate for peace, I decided to write down the recipe for Rachael. After gathering advice from family and friends, and testing and tasting ten batches, I distilled a formula for classic hummus, one that made my mother proud. —*Alia Yunis*

# Hummus with Tahini

*Hummus B'Tahina*

The building blocks of this most popular of Mediterranean *mezes*, or small plates, couldn't be simpler: chickpeas, sesame paste, lemon juice, garlic, and not much more. Yet these few ingredients can yield incredibly nuanced flavors and a sumptuous texture, and versions vary in subtle and not-so-subtle ways from family to family, kitchen to kitchen, country to country.

| | |
|---|---|
| 5 | oz. dried chickpeas |
| 1 | tsp. baking soda |
| 6 | cloves garlic, crushed |
| 1¼ | cups plus 3½ tbsp. tahini |
| ½ | cup plus 2 tbsp. fresh lemon juice |
| | Kosher salt, to taste |
| 2 | tbsp. extra-virgin olive oil, plus more for garnish |
| ⅛ | tsp. sumac or paprika, for garnish |
| 1 | tsp. finely chopped flat-leaf parsley, for garnish |
| | Sliced pickles, for garnish |
| | Pita, for serving |

*Makes 4 cups*

**1.** In a medium bowl, combine chickpeas with 6 cups cold water and stir in baking soda; cover and let soak overnight. Drain chickpeas, transfer to a 2-qt. saucepan, and cover with 6 cups fresh water. Cover and bring to a boil over medium-high heat and cook until very tender, 40–50 minutes. Remove pan from heat and let cool slightly.

**2.** Drain chickpeas, reserving cooking liquid. To the bowl of a food processor, add chickpeas and 5 cloves garlic and process for

about 2 minutes. Add ¾ cup of the cooking liquid, along with 1¼ cups tahini, ½ cup lemon juice, and 2 tbsp. olive oil; season with salt. Process, stopping occasionally to scrape down the sides of the bowl, until the mixture is very smooth, about 8 minutes. Cover with plastic wrap; refrigerate until flavors have melded, about 4 hours.

**3.** Bring hummus to room temperature. Finely chop the remaining clove of garlic and sprinkle with salt. Using the side of a knife, scrape the garlic against the work surface while chopping occasionally to make a paste; set aside. In a small bowl whisk together the remaining tahini, lemon juice, 3½ tbsp. ice water, and the garlic paste until the mixture is creamy; season with salt and set aside.

**4.** To serve, place hummus in a bowl and make a small indentation in the middle using the back of a spoon. Pour the reserved tahini mixture into the indentation and garnish hummus with olive oil, sumac or paprika, parsley, and pickles. Serve with pita.

# Soups and Stews

First, you brown some onions, celery, and bacon. Next, you pour in stock or water and maybe a little wine, scraping up the flavorful caramelized bits before adding meat or vegetables. Then you stir, season, taste, and wait. As the pot simmers and your kitchen fills with aromas, sharp flavors mellow and subtle ones intensify, until it all comes together in a beautiful union. Creamy corn chowder, French onion soup bubbling beneath gooey Gruyère, Polish pork and sauerkraut stew—such dishes feed the soul, warm the body, and leave us content.

*A student at Le Ferrandi culinary school in Paris tends to a simmering pot of veal stock under the watchful eye of his professor.*

# Burgundy-Style Beef Stew
*Boeuf à la Bourguignonne*

There are many ways to say "beef stew" in French. In Provence, you might ask for *daube*; in Belgium, it's called *carbonnade* and is made with dark beer. But the most famous of these regional stews is Burgundy's, made with red wine and cooked slowly, until the flavors fully meld and the beef becomes meltingly tender.

| | |
|---|---|
| 8 | oz. slab bacon, cut into ½-inch slices and cut crosswise into ¼-inch pieces |
| 2 | tbsp. canola oil |
| 2½ | lbs. trimmed boneless beef chuck, cut into 2-inch cubes |
| | Kosher salt and freshly ground black pepper, to taste |
| 1 | large carrot, roughly chopped |
| 1 | large yellow onion, roughly chopped |
| 1 | rib celery, roughly chopped |
| 2 | tbsp. tomato paste |
| 3 | cloves garlic, roughly chopped |
| ¼ | cup flour |
| 2 | cups beef or veal stock |
| 1 | 750-ml. bottle full-bodied red wine, such as merlot |
| 1 | bouquet garni (1 sprig each parsley and thyme and 1 bay leaf, tied together with kitchen twine) |
| 2 | tbsp. unsalted butter |
| 10 | oz. button mushrooms, stemmed and quartered |
| 32 | pearl onions, peeled |
| ¼ | cup flat-leaf parsley leaves, for garnish |

*Serves 8*

1. Heat the oven to 325°F. Cook the bacon in an 8-qt. Dutch oven over medium heat, stirring occasionally, until browned and crisp, about 20 minutes. Using a slotted spoon, transfer the bacon to a paper towel–lined plate; pour off all but 2 tbsp. of the rendered fat.

2. Increase the heat to medium-high and add the oil to the Dutch oven. Working in batches, add the beef, season with salt and pepper, and cook, turning occasionally, until the beef is browned on all sides, 5–6 minutes. Transfer the beef to a plate and set aside. Add the carrots, onions, and celery and cook, stirring occasionally, until onions are soft and browned, about 7 minutes. Stir in the tomato paste and garlic and cook for 1 minute. Return the beef to the pot along with any juices, sprinkle with flour, and stir until the ingredients are well coated with flour. Add the stock, wine, and bouquet garni. Cover, transfer to the oven, and cook until the beef is tender, 2½–3 hours.

3. Meanwhile, melt 1 tbsp. butter in a 12-inch skillet over medium-high heat. Add the mushrooms and cook, stirring occasionally, until the mushrooms are soft and

golden brown, 10–12 minutes. Transfer the mushrooms to a bowl and set aside.

4. Add 1 tbsp. butter to the skillet along with the pearl onions and 2 tbsp. water. Cover partially and cook until the water evaporates and the onions are tender, about 4 minutes. Uncover and continue cooking the onions, stirring occasionally, until browned all over, 2–3 minutes more. Transfer onions to the bowl with the mushrooms and cover to keep warm.

5. Remove the beef from the oven. Using a slotted spoon, transfer the beef to a large bowl and cover to keep warm. Set a fine mesh strainer over a 4-qt. saucepan. Strain the cooking liquid, discarding solids, and bring to a boil over medium-high heat; cook until reduced and thick enough to coat the back of a spoon, 10–12 minutes. Season sauce with salt and pepper.

6. To serve, divide the reserved beef between 8 serving bowls and pour some sauce over each serving. Divide the bacon, mushrooms, and pearl onions evenly between the bowls, and garnish with the parsley leaves. Serve with crusty bread, if you like.

# Creamy Corn Chowder

The recipe for this summer chowder comes from the Murphy family of Cape Breton, Nova Scotia (their home is pictured at right during a late-summer party). Matriarch Eva Murphy, a home cook who harvests many of the ingredients for the soup from her own vegetable patch, scrapes sweet corn off the cob and thickens the soup by puréeing a little of the chowder and stirring it back into the pot.

| | |
|---|---|
| 8 | ears fresh corn, shucked |
| 8 | strips bacon, chopped |
| 4 | tbsp. unsalted butter |
| 1 | tbsp. minced fresh thyme |
| 4 | cloves garlic, minced |
| 2 | ribs celery, minced |
| 1 | medium yellow onion, minced |
| 1 | bay leaf |
| 6 | cups milk |
| 3 | medium new potatoes (about 1½ lbs.), peeled and cut into ½-inch cubes |
| | Kosher salt and freshly ground black pepper, to taste |
| ¼ | cup thinly sliced fresh basil, for garnish |

*Serves 8*

**1.** Working over a large bowl, slice the kernels off the corn cobs, scraping the cobs with the knife to extract the flavorful juices. Halve 5 of the bare corn cobs crosswise, discarding the rest. Set the corn and cobs aside.

**2.** Heat the bacon in a 6-qt. pot over medium heat and cook, stirring occasionally, until crisp, about 12 minutes. Reserve 3 tbsp. bacon for a garnish, leaving the remaining bacon and fat in the pot. Add the butter, thyme, garlic, celery, onions, and bay leaf. Cover the pot and cook, stirring occasionally, until the onions soften, about 6 minutes. Add the reserved corn kernels and cobs, milk, and potatoes. Cover, bring the chowder to a boil, reduce heat to low, and simmer, stirring occasionally, until the potatoes are tender, about 25 minutes. Skim any foam from the surface of the soup.

**3.** Discard the cobs and bay leaf; transfer 1½ cups of the soup to a blender and purée. Stir the purée back into the chowder to thicken it. Season with salt and pepper and serve the soup garnished with the reserved bacon and basil.

**COOKING NOTE** *Here are two other methods for slicing corn kernels off the cob: Lay the cob horizontally on the cutting board to cut off the kernels. Or, firmly hold the cob vertically, resting the bottom on the cutting board, and slice off the kernels from the bottom half first, then turn the cob and hold the opposite end as you slice off the kernels from the other half.*

# German Split Pea Soup

*Erbsensuppe*

SAVEUR editor Todd Coleman fell in love with this fragrant split pea soup as a child in Germany. The addition of a little flour gives it a smooth texture, while celery root adds an earthy note.

| | |
|---|---|
| 2 | tbsp. extra-virgin olive oil |
| 2 | slices bacon, minced |
| 1 | large onion, minced |
| 1 | rib celery, minced |
| 1 | large carrot, peeled and minced |
| 1 | small celery root, peeled and minced |
| | Kosher salt, to taste |
| 2 | tbsp. flour |
| 10 | sprigs flat-leaf parsley |
| 8 | sprigs fresh thyme |
| 2 | bay leaves |
| 1 | lb. green split peas, rinsed and drained |
| 2 | large smoked ham hocks (about 2 lbs. total) |
| | Freshly ground black pepper, to taste |

*Serves 4*

**1.** Put the oil and bacon into a 6-qt. pot and cook over medium-high heat until crisp, about 6 minutes. Using a slotted spoon, transfer the bacon to a paper towel–lined plate; set aside. Add onions, celery, carrots, and celery root, season with salt, and cook, stirring occasionally, until soft, about 10 minutes. Stir in flour; cook, stirring, for 3 minutes.

**2.** Tie the parsley, thyme, and bay leaves together with kitchen twine; add to the pot along with the peas, ham hocks, and 7 cups water. Bring to a boil over high heat. Reduce heat to medium-low and simmer, covered, until peas are very tender, about 1 hour. Remove from heat. Discard herbs. Transfer hocks to a plate and let cool; pull off and chop the meat; discard fat, skin, and bones. Stir meat into the soup, season with salt and pepper, and ladle the soup into bowls. Sprinkle with reserved bacon.

## Comfort Bowl

The year my family moved to Germany, my dad booked us a bus trip into the Taunus Mountains, north of Frankfurt—an adventure that included dinner and the chance to chop down our own Christmas tree. The excursion did not begin auspiciously. Mom, Dad, my then three-year-old brother, Casey (that's him on the left in the photo below; I'm in the Superman pj's), and I piled into the car, but when Dad

turned the key, the engine wouldn't start. We made it to the bus just as it was about to depart. Three hours later, we arrived at our destination. We had to trudge deep into the woods, hungry and cold, to find a worthy specimen. A dose of salvation arrived hours later when we stopped off at a guesthouse for dinner and were served *erbsensuppe*, a nourishing split pea soup. Each smoky spoonful warmed our bodies and revived our spirits. —*Todd Coleman*

# French Onion Soup

*Soupe à l'Oignon*

The first step to making this brasserie classic is slowly braising onions with sherry and butter until they are luxuriously soft and intensely flavorful. Rich veal stock and a browned and bubbly layer of Gruyère further enrich the luscious soup, a favorite at the Paris brasserie Au Pied de Cochon (pictured at right); this recipe is based on theirs. To make it, you'll need six ovenproof ceramic bowls.

| | |
|---|---|
| 1 | cup white wine |
| ½ | cup plus 3 tbsp. sherry |
| 10 | tbsp. unsalted butter |
| 1 | tsp. sugar |
| 3 | large yellow onions, thinly sliced |
| | Kosher salt and freshly ground black pepper, to taste |
| 6 | sprigs flat-leaf parsley |
| 6 | sprigs fresh thyme |
| 2 | bay leaves |
| 2 | qts. beef or veal stock |
| 12 | ½-inch-thick slices baguette |
| 2 | cloves garlic, smashed |
| 6 | cups grated Gruyère |
| 2 | cups finely grated Parmigiano-Reggiano |
| 2 | tsp. minced flat-leaf parsley for garnish, optional |

*Serves 6*

**1.** Heat the oven to 425°F. Combine the wine, ½ cup sherry, 8 tbsp. butter, sugar, onions, and salt and pepper in a 9 x 13-inch casserole dish and cook, uncovered, stirring occasionally, until the onions just begin to brown, about 40 minutes. Cover casserole with foil and continue braising, stirring occasionally, until onions are caramelized, about 1 hour more. Set onions aside and keep warm.

**2.** Meanwhile, tie the parsley, thyme, and bay leaves together with kitchen twine to make a bouquet garni. Put the herb bundle and stock into a stockpot and bring to a boil. Reduce the heat to medium-low and simmer, partially covered, for 30 minutes.

Remove and discard the bouquet garni. Stir in the remaining sherry and cook for 5 minutes more.

**3.** While the broth simmers, spread the baguette slices with the remaining butter. Toast in a skillet over medium heat, turning once, until golden, 5–7 minutes total. Rub the slices generously with the garlic cloves and set aside. Discard any remaining garlic.

**4.** Heat a broiler and place the rack 6 inches from the heating element. Arrange 6 heat-proof bowls on a foil-lined baking sheet, divide the onions and broth between the bowls, and stir together. Place 2 baguette slices in each bowl and top each with about 1 cup Gruyère and about ⅓ cup Parmigiano-Reggiano. Broil until the cheeses are browned and bubbly, about 4 minutes. Serve the soup garnished with minced parsley, if you like.

# Matzo Ball Soup

In Jewish households around the country, chicken soup is so closely associated with comfort and well-being that it has earned the nickname Jewish penicillin. With the addition of matzo balls, it is often served at the Passover meal. This recipe comes from SAVEUR contributor Pamela Renner, who adds a little seltzer or club soda to the matzo balls to ensure that they turn out light and airy.

| | |
|---|---|
| 12 | sprigs fresh dill |
| 3 | sprigs fresh cilantro |
| 4 | cloves garlic, thinly sliced |
| 2 | small yellow onions, thinly sliced |
| 1 | bunch celery, cut into ½-inch pieces |
| | Sprigs from ½ bunch flat-leaf parsley, plus 1 tbsp. chopped |
| 3 | large carrots, peeled and cut into ½-inch pieces |
| 1 | turnip, peeled and cut into ½-inch pieces |
| 1 | parsnip, cut into ½-inch pieces |
| 1 | 3½-lb. whole chicken |
| 1 | lb. chicken feet (optional) |
| | Salt, to taste |
| 2 | tbsp. seltzer or club soda |
| ⅛ | tsp. dried dill |
| 2 | eggs, at room temperature |
| ½ | cup plus 1 tbsp. matzo meal |

*Serves 8–10*

**1.** Gather the fresh dill, cilantro, garlic cloves, onions, celery, and parsley sprigs in a piece of cheese-cloth to form a purse; secure with twine. Make a second purse with the carrots, turnips, and parsnips.

**2.** Put the dill purse, chicken, chicken feet, salt, and 1½ gallons of water into a large pot and bring to a boil. Reduce the heat to medium-low and simmer, covered, for about 1½ hours. Add the carrot purse and simmer gently, covered, until the carrots are tender, about 30 minutes.

**3.** Remove and discard the dill purse and chicken feet. Transfer the chicken and carrot purse to a plate and let cool. Pull enough breast meat into fine shreds to make ¾ cup. Reserve 1 cup of the vegetables from the carrot purse. Cover and chill the shredded chicken and vegetables. (Reserve the remaining chicken and vegetables for another use.) Set a fine mesh sieve over a large bowl and strain the broth; chill overnight. Skim off and discard all but 2 tbsp. chicken fat from broth; set fat aside.

**4.** Whisk together the reserved chicken fat, club soda, dried dill, and eggs in a bowl. Pour in the matzo meal while whisking. Cover and chill the matzo mixture for 15 minutes.

**5.** Bring 2½ qts. salted water to a boil over high heat. With wet hands, form the matzo mixture into 1-inch balls. Reduce the heat to medium and drop in the matzo balls. Cook, covered, for about 15 minutes. Stir the matzo balls gently and simmer, covered, until fluffy, about 10 minutes more.

**6.** Meanwhile, transfer the reserved shredded chicken, vegetables, and broth to a large pot and heat over medium heat. Transfer the matzo balls to the broth. Serve the soup garnished with chopped parsley, if you like.

## Hot Stuff

Chili powder is to Texas what peanut butter is to jelly: you can't think of one without the other. With its deep red color and robust aroma, chili powder is the very essence of Tex-Mex food, seasoning everything from the meat for chilies and tacos to the sauce for enchiladas. The powder is made from seemingly mundane ingredients—dried chiles (usually ancho), oregano, cumin, garlic, and, sometimes, salt—that, when processed together, make a substance whose properties are nothing short of magical. Chili powder disperses its color and potent flavor when fried in oil or grease, melding with the beef and tomatoes in a pot of chili to create its distinctive taste and look. Rubbed onto a steak before grilling, it lends a striking hue and char. Chili powder was invented in Texas; by whom is a matter of some dispute. The chili historian Joe Cooper maintains that a German immigrant named William Gebhardt invented the first chili powder in 1896 in the town of New Braunfels, which lies between Austin and San Antonio. Gebhardt operated a café in the back of a place called Miller's Saloon and devised a way of pulverizing Mexican dried chiles using a meat grinder (probably in an adaptation of the Hungarian method for making paprika). He sold his new product as "Tampico Dust" but later changed the name to Gebhardt's Eagle Chili Powder, as it is still called today.

# Woody DeSilva's Championship Chili

In Texas, chili is practically a religion—and by chili Texans mean cubed beef chuck simmered for hours with tomatoes and chili powder and then thickened with masa harina (corn flour). Don't even think about adding beans. Each year, scores of the faithful converge in the town of Terlingua, Texas, for the mother of all chili cook-offs; this recipe, created by home cook Woody DeSilva, took first prize in 1968.

| | |
|---|---|
| 4 | lbs. beef chuck, trimmed and cut into ½-inch cubes |
| | Kosher salt and freshly ground black pepper, to taste |
| 4 | tbsp. canola oil |
| 5 | medium onions, chopped |
| 5 | cloves garlic, minced |
| 2 | 6-oz. cans tomato paste |
| 4 | tbsp. dried oregano |
| 3 | tbsp. chili powder |
| 4 | tsp. ground chile pequín or cayenne pepper |
| 1 | tbsp. sweet paprika |
| 1 | tbsp. Tabasco |
| 1 | tsp. ground cumin |
| 4 | tbsp. masa harina |

*Serves 6*

**1.** Season the beef with salt and pepper. Heat the oil in a 6-qt. pot over high heat. Working in 4 batches, brown the beef, about 3 minutes per batch. Using a slotted spoon, transfer the beef to a plate.

**2.** Add the onions and garlic to the pot, reserving a few tablespoonfuls of chopped onion for garnish. Cook, stirring, until golden brown, about 5 minutes. Return the beef to the pot, stir in the tomato paste, and cook, stirring frequently and scraping the bottom of the pot with a wooden spoon, until the tomato paste is caramelized, 10–12 minutes. Add the oregano, chili powder, chile pequín, paprika, Tabasco, and cumin; cook, stirring frequently, for 1 minute.

**3.** Add 5 cups water to the chili and bring to a boil. Reduce heat to medium-low and simmer, stirring occasionally, until the meat is tender, about 2 hours.

**4.** Stir the masa harina into the chili, season with salt, and simmer, stirring, until thickened, about 5 minutes. Ladle into serving bowls and garnish with the reserved onions, if you like.

# Thai Hot and Sour Shrimp Soup

*Tom Yum Goong*

Fragrant with lime juice and lemongrass, this hot and sour soup is served throughout Thailand, with subtle regional variations in heat, sweetness, and pungency. Pictured at left are Wai Smitaman and his wife, Kiew Krislas, a home cook in southern Thailand who provided the recipe upon which this one was based.

| | |
|---|---|
| 3 | large stalks fresh lemongrass |
| 4 | cups chicken stock |
| 12 | fresh or frozen Kaffir lime leaves |
| 1 | cup canned straw mushrooms, drained |
| 2–4 | tbsp. roasted Thai chile paste (nam prik pao) |
| 8 | oz. medium shrimp, peeled and deveined |
| 1½ | tbsp. fish sauce |
| 4–6 | Thai chiles, stemmed and smashed with side of a knife |
| 3 | scallions, cut into 1-inch lengths |
| | Juice of 1 lime |
| 2 | cups cooked rice (optional) |

*Serves 2*

**1.** Trim tip and root ends of lemongrass stalks and remove and discard tough outer layer. Using a meat mallet or the side of a knife, smash lemongrass to flatten it; tie stalks into a knot; set aside. Pour stock into a 2-qt. saucepan and bring to a boil. Add lemongrass and half the lime leaves, reduce heat to medium-low, and simmer until fragrant, about 5 minutes.

**2.** Remove and discard lemongrass and lime leaves and increase heat to high. Stir in mushrooms and chile paste, to taste, and boil for 1 minute; add shrimp and fish sauce and cook until shrimp are just cooked through, about 45 seconds. Combine remaining lime leaves with chiles, scallions, and lime juice in a serving bowl or tureen. Ladle soup into serving bowl, stir, and serve immediately, with rice, if you like.

## Big World

For my 13th-birthday dinner, my parents and I drove from our home in Falmouth, Massachusetts, to Boston to eat at a popular Thai restaurant called the King and I. This was a big deal. We didn't go to Boston often and we'd never eaten Thai food. In small-town Massachusetts at that time, the brick oven pizzeria was as urbane as it got. The place was bright and loud and packed. The waiter came over and we each ordered pad Thai—the noodles were enough like pasta to assuage my father, who would rather have been at a red-sauce joint—plus a bowl of *tom yum* soup for me, which I chose because it included shrimp. The soup arrived first, a brown crock of cloudy broth with a few mushrooms, a sprig of cilantro, flecks of chopped something (lemongrass and Kaffir lime leaf, I would later learn), and just one pink shrimp. No matter; it was the broth that floored me. It had an unfamiliar sourness that was round and sweet, but it also had an intriguing fishy flavor and a beautiful citrusy fragrance. Then the pad Thai arrived, a heap of rice noodles tangled with stir-fried egg and scallion, sprinkled with peanuts, all of it strange to me and addictive. I remember looking around to see how the other diners used chopsticks, and then back at my quiet family who twirled our noodles around forks. After that meal, I'd sit in algebra class and dream of *tom yum*, the memory of its tartness making my mouth water. I'd spend weekends making pad Thai for my friends, once I realized that the "international foods" section of the Stop & Shop carried fish sauce. That soup made me lust for places like New York City, where surely everyone ate things like Thai food every night. And when I finally moved there—and realized that they didn't—I felt at home anyway. *—Sarah DiGregorio*

# Tuscan-Style Kale Soup

*Ribollita*

The Italian name for this soup—*ribollita*, which literally means reboiled—reveals its very practical origins as a way to use leftover vegetables and day-old bread. Long simmering renders the beans tender and the kale silky; hunks of rustic bread all but disappear, thickening the broth to a stewlike consistency. Flavorful and sustaining, the sum of these humble parts is a masterpiece of Tuscan peasant cooking.

¼ cup extra-virgin olive oil, plus 3 tbsp. for serving
½ cup chopped flat-leaf parsley
6 ribs celery, chopped
4 cloves garlic, chopped
3 medium carrots, chopped
1 small red onion, chopped
Kosher salt and freshly ground black pepper, to taste
1 28-oz. can whole peeled tomatoes, undrained
2 lbs. trimmed and roughly chopped kale or cavolo nero (see Cooking Note)
3 14-oz. cans borlotti or cannellini beans, drained
1 ¾-lb. loaf stale ciabatta bread, trimmed of crust and torn into 1-inch pieces

*Serves 8–10*

1. Heat ¼ cup oil in an 8-qt. pot over medium-high heat. Add the parsley, celery, garlic, carrots, and onion and season with salt and pepper. Cook, stirring occasionally, until vegetables are golden brown, 15–20 minutes.

2. Put the tomatoes into a medium bowl. Crush the tomatoes by hand and transfer to the pot along with the juices. Reduce the heat to medium-low and cook until thickened, 25–30 minutes. Add the kale, 2 cans of beans, and 16 cups water. Bring to a boil, reduce heat to medium-low, and simmer, uncovered, until the kale is tender, about 30 minutes.

3. Meanwhile, purée the remaining can of beans and ½ cup of water in a blender. Stir into the pot. Add the bread pieces and remaining oil. Cook, stirring occasionally, until thick, about 30 minutes. Season with salt and pepper and serve soup drizzled with olive oil.

**COOKING NOTE** Ribollita *can be made with any type of kale, but cavolo nero, a Tuscan variety that grows through the lean winter months, maintains its body and crinkly texture particularly well. In the United States, cavolo nero is also known as dinosaur kale, Tuscan kale, and lacinato kale.*

# Smoked Pork and Sauerkraut Stew

*Bigos*

The extravagant pork and sauerkraut stew called *bigos* may be our favorite from Poland's wide repertoire of hearty pork dishes. Thick with smoked pork shoulder, pork butt, bacon, and kielbasa, this version is based on one made by Stella Bobak, whose family owns the Chicago supermarket Bobak's, a venerable emporium of Polish products and pork in every imaginable cut and cure.

| | |
|---|---|
| ¼ | oz. dried porcini mushrooms |
| ¼ | lb. smoked bacon, cut into 1-inch pieces |
| 2 | oz. fatback, cut into ½-inch cubes |
| ½ | lb. boneless pork butt, cut into 1-inch pieces |
| ½ | lb. smoked kielbasa, cut into 1-inch pieces |
| ⅓ | lb. smoked pork shoulder, cut into 1-inch pieces |
| 6 | whole allspice |
| 2 | bay leaves |
| 2 | large yellow onions, chopped |
| 6 | tbsp. tomato paste |
| 1 | tbsp. flour |
| 4 | lbs. sauerkraut, roughly chopped and rinsed |
| ½ | cup red wine |
| 6 | cups beef or veal stock |
| | Salt and freshly ground black pepper, to taste |
| | Chopped flat-leaf parsley, for garnish |

*Serves 8*

**1.** Put the dried mushrooms and 1½ cups water into a bowl and let soften for 1 hour. Drain and reserve water.

**2.** Heat the oven to 350°F. Cook the bacon and fatback in a large pot over medium heat until crisp, 8–10 minutes. Using a slotted spoon, transfer the bacon and fatback to a plate. Add the pork butt, kielbasa, and pork shoulder to the pot and increase heat to medium-high; cook, turning meat occasionally, until the meat is browned, 12–14 minutes. Using a slotted spoon, transfer the meat to a plate and set aside.

**3.** Add the allspice, bay leaves, and onions to the pot and cook, scraping up browned bits, until softened, 8–10 minutes. Add the tomato paste and cook until browned, 8–10 minutes. Add the flour and cook for about 2 minutes. Add the mushrooms and sauerkraut to the pot and cook for about 12 minutes. Add the mushroom water; the bacon and fatback; the pork butt, kielbasa, and pork shoulder; the wine; and the stock and bring to a boil. Season with salt and pepper. Cover the pot with foil and a tight-fitting lid and braise in the oven until the meat is very tender, about 1 hour. Divide the stew between bowls, garnish with parsley, and serve.

## City of Pork

Hog heaven is the deli counter at Bobak's, the Polish supermarket on Chicago's Southwest side. There you can find the world's best bacon, double-smoked and meaty, with ribbons of aromatic fat that melt on your tongue; dozens of varieties of kielbasa dangling from hooks, some thick and reddish with crinkled rinds, others in slender loops; not to mention all the smoked hams and loins and ribs and

more. Not surprisingly, this store started life as a smokehouse; after Stan Bobak emigrated from the Highland region of Poland in the 1960s, he worked in the city's stockyards and started smoking sausage on the side. Now the business is as beloved for its home style cooking as it is for its cured meat; on my last trip to Bobak's in-store restaurant, I ate an unforgettable bowl of *bigos* along with crêpes filled with shredded pork, mini aspics studded with herbs and ham, and bacon-wrapped pork loin. Ah, the joys of lunch at a butcher shop! —*Dana Bowen*

CAUTION

EXHAUST FAN MUST BE
TURNED ON BEFORE
LIGHTING COOKING APPLIANCES

WAFFLE
HOUSE

EDDIE

MASTER GRILL OP

M MEMBER SINCE 20

# Eggs

It's our favorite way to greet the day: a farm-fresh egg fried in olive oil until the white is crisp around the edges and the yolk is barely firm. A little coarse sea salt, a grind of black pepper, a thick slice of crusty bread, and the morning is off to a blissful start. Other times, we ask more of this elemental ingredient, whether poached and covered in hollandaise, smothered with a bright tomato salsa, or baked into a frittata topped with ricotta. So indispensable is the egg to our well-being that calling it the perfect food almost seems like an understatement.

*A line cook at the Waffle House in East Point, Georgia.*

# Ricotta and Roasted Pepper Frittata

*Frittata con Ricotta e Peperoni*

Main-course frittatas like this one are popular in the southern Italian region of Calabria, where traditional sheep farming is an enduring way of life and freshly made sheep's milk ricotta is an everyday pleasure. Calabrians sometimes add sliced cured sausage to this ricotta frittata on Easter, to celebrate the end of the Lenten fast.

½ cup freshly grated
  Pecorino Romano

2 tbsp. roughly chopped
  flat-leaf parsley

1½ tsp. kosher salt

1 tsp. chopped fresh oregano

8 eggs, beaten
  Freshly ground black
  pepper, to taste

3 tbsp. extra-virgin olive oil

1 large yellow onion, halved
  and thinly sliced

1 small new potato, peeled
  and sliced into ⅛-inch
  rounds

1 medium red bell pepper,
  roasted, peeled, and cut
  into ¼-inch strips

¾ cup ricotta cheese

*Serves 4–6*

**1.** Arrange a rack in the middle of the oven and heat oven to 425°F. In a large bowl, whisk together ¼ cup of the Pecorino, the parsley, ½ tsp. salt, oregano, and eggs and season with black pepper. Set the egg mixture aside.

**2.** Heat the oil in a 10-inch nonstick ovenproof skillet over medium-high heat. Add the remaining salt and the onions and potatoes and cook, stirring occasionally, until lightly browned and soft, about 20 minutes.

**3.** Remove the skillet from the heat. Add the egg mixture to the skillet and stir to distribute the onions and potatoes evenly. Scatter the peppers over the top, spoon the ricotta over the mixture in 6 dollops, and sprinkle with the remaining Pecorino. Bake until the frittata is lightly browned on top and the center is set, about 15 minutes. Run a rubber spatula around the edges of the frittata to loosen it, then slide it onto a serving plate. Season with more black pepper, if you like, cut into wedges, and serve.

Many years ago, when I was a private chef, I was asked one morning to prepare eggs Benedict for breakfast. No problem, I thought. But when I dropped the first egg into the simmering water, it spread out into an amorphous mess. Same thing on the next try. What was I doing wrong? I called my friend Ted MacLeod, an expert brunch cook. "The secret to poaching eggs," Ted told me, "is in the amount of vinegar you use. The right amount coaxes them into firmness." I tried his method—a half cup of white distilled vinegar and a half teaspoon of salt in four cups of water—and, sure enough, my poached eggs came out beautifully. Months afterward, though, I ran into another problem. I was using a skillet to poach eggs; when I dropped the eggs into the water they flattened into dispiriting disks. Thinking that the outcome might have something to do with the water's depth, I switched to a tall pot, and—voilà!—the eggs gracefully formed into appealing orbs. Another egg-poaching tip I picked up along the way: cracking each egg into a small bowl or teacup before pouring it into the simmering water helps the eggs maintain a more compact shape.
—*Todd Coleman*

# Classic Eggs Benedict

No one knows for sure where the name "eggs Benedict" came from, but most accounts trace this dish's invention to Delmonico's, an iconic Gilded Age restaurant in New York City. It has since become an American brunch classic, and no wonder. The combination of poached eggs, creamy hollandaise, and Canadian bacon on a toasted English muffin manages to be elegant and comforting at the same time.

2      cups distilled white vinegar
2½     tsp. kosher salt, plus
       more to taste
1      tbsp. canola oil
8      slices Canadian bacon
3      egg yolks
1      tbsp. plus 1 tsp. fresh
       lemon juice
¼      tsp. Tabasco
8      tbsp. unsalted butter,
       melted
8      eggs, cracked into separate
       small bowls
4      English muffins, split and
       lightly toasted
       Paprika or cayenne pepper,
       for garnish

*Serves 4*

**1.** Bring 16 cups of water to a boil in a tall 6-qt. saucepan over high heat. Add the vinegar and 2 tsp. salt, lower heat to medium, and bring to a simmer.

**2.** Heat the oil in a 12-inch skillet over medium-high heat. Add the bacon and cook, turning once, until lightly browned, about 3 minutes. Remove the skillet from the heat.

**3.** Combine the egg yolks, lemon juice, Tabasco, 4 tsp. warm water, and the remaining salt in a blender. Blend at medium speed while slowly drizzling in the melted butter to make the hollandaise. Transfer to a bowl, cover with foil, and set aside.

**4.** Swirl the simmering vinegar water with a spoon to create a whirlpool. Carefully slide each egg into the water and poach until just firm, about 3 minutes. Using a slotted spoon, transfer the eggs to a paper towel–lined plate.

**5.** Divide the toasted muffin halves between 4 plates and top each half with 1 slice of the reserved bacon and 1 poached egg. Spoon about 3 tbsp. hollandaise over each egg, sprinkle with paprika or cayenne, and serve.

# Eggs Poached in Spicy Tomato Sauce

*Shakshuka*

In Jerusalem's Mahane Yehuda market (pictured at left), this spicy tomato stew dotted with poached eggs is a popular breakfast item at many food stalls. We think it makes a satisfying meal at any time of the day, especially with warm pita bread to sop up the thick sauce and rich egg yolks.

¼ cup extra-virgin olive oil
5 Anaheim chiles or
   3 jalapeños, stemmed,
   seeded, and minced
1 small yellow onion,
   chopped
8 cloves garlic, crushed
1 tbsp. paprika
1 tsp. ground cumin
1 28-oz. can whole peeled
   tomatoes, undrained
   Kosher salt, to taste
8 eggs
½ cup crumbled feta cheese
1 tbsp. chopped flat-leaf
   parsley
   Warm pita bread,
   for serving

*Serves 4–6*

**1.** Heat oil in a 12-inch skillet over medium-high heat. Add chiles and onions and cook, stirring occasionally, until soft and golden brown, about 6 minutes. Add garlic, paprika, and cumin and cook, stirring frequently, until garlic is soft, about 2 minutes more. Put tomatoes and their liquid into a medium bowl and crush well with your hands. Add crushed tomatoes and their liquid to skillet along with ½ cup water, reduce heat to medium, and simmer, stirring occasionally, until thickened slightly, about 20 minutes. Season sauce with salt.

**2.** Crack eggs over sauce so that eggs are evenly distributed across sauce's surface. Cover skillet and cook until yolks are just set, about 5 minutes. Using a spoon, baste the whites of the eggs with tomato mixture, being careful not to disturb the yolk. Sprinkle *shakshuka* with feta and parsley and serve hot with pita bread, for dipping.

## Best Breakfast

I first stumbled on La Abeja, a little Mexican café on Figueroa Street in the Los Angeles neighborhood of Highland Park, in 1986, when I was 23 (that's me, pictured below on the left, right around that time). My best friend, Joyce, lived in nearby Mount Washington, and we started making an almost religious ritual out of meeting there Saturday mornings to go over in penitential detail all the silly, alcohol-fueled

things we'd done the night before. Boy, did those breakfasts hit the spot: huevos rancheros served with fluffy Mexican rice and some of the best refried beans in the world; big, hot bowls of *menudo* studded with tender tripe and hominy; and endless cups of soul-satisfying, diner-variety coffee. La Abeja (or The Bee) serves Mexican home-style cooking of the

highest order; not surprising considering that the place started its life as a corner store in 1969 with a kitchen in the back where the owners, Jose and Gloria Fonseca, would prepare meals for their family. Eventually, customers started asking whether they could get take-out versions of some of those foods, many of them made from recipes the family had brought from their native Mexico City. Before long the Fonsecas cleared out the aisles and shelves and set up tables and chairs (they kept the candy counter up front). When I visited La Abeja recently, I hadn't been back in over a decade. I was sad to learn that the Fonsecas had passed away, but relieved to find their son Roy at the helm. After all those years, very little had changed. Neighborhood kids were stopping in for a pack of Bubble Yum; sleepy-eyed art students and guys from the auto body shop down the street filled the tables; and the *platillo de huevos rancheros* that I ordered was still the most fortifying breakfast around. —*James Oseland*

# Huevos Rancheros

This recipe for huevos rancheros, the gorgeous mess of fried eggs smothered in a spicy tomato sauce, came from La Abeja, a café in Los Angeles where the Fonseca family has been serving up Mexican home-style cooking for decades. Traditionally a cowboy's breakfast served over warm corn tortillas with rice and refried beans, the dish has become a fixture in diners on both sides of the border.

| | |
|---|---|
| 14 | plum tomatoes, cored |
| 12 | tbsp. canola oil |
| 3 | cloves garlic, minced |
| ½ | jalapeño, stemmed and minced |
| ½ | medium yellow onion, chopped |
| 1 | tbsp. fresh lime juice<br>Kosher salt and freshly ground black pepper, to taste |
| 8 | corn tortillas |
| 8 | eggs<br>Pickled jalapeño slices, for garnish |

*Serves 4*

**1.** Heat a 12-inch cast-iron skillet over high heat. Add the tomatoes and cook, turning, until the skins blacken, 8–10 minutes. Peel the tomatoes, purée in a blender, strain through a sieve, and set aside.

**2.** Heat 4 tbsp. oil in a 4-qt. pan over medium heat. Add the garlic, jalapeños, and onions and cook until soft, 6–8 minutes. Add the tomato purée and bring to a boil. Stir in the lime juice and season with salt and pepper. Remove from the heat and set aside.

**3.** Working in 4 batches, heat 1 tbsp. oil in a 12-inch nonstick skillet over medium-high heat. Add 2 tortillas to the skillet and cook, flipping once, until warmed, about 20 seconds. Repeat with the remaining tortillas.

**4.** Divide the tortillas between 4 plates. Working in 2 batches, heat the remaining oil in the same skillet over medium heat and fry the eggs to desired doneness. Top each tortilla with a fried egg and tomato sauce. Garnish with pickled jalapeño slices and serve.

# Matzo Brei with Mushrooms and Asparagus

Simple and soulful, this scramble of eggs and matzo is a breakfast staple in many Jewish households, particularly during the Passover holiday, when leavened breads are off limits. We've added sautéed mushrooms and asparagus, but you could just as well leave them out and serve the matzo brei as you might pancakes or French toast, with a topping of jam or maple syrup.

8   asparagus tips
4   tbsp. unsalted butter
8   cremini mushrooms, stemmed and cut into sixths
    Kosher salt and freshly ground black pepper, to taste
3   6-inch square pieces matzo
5   eggs, lightly beaten
1   tbsp. minced flat-leaf parsley, for garnish (optional)

*Serves 2*

**1.** Bring 8 cups of water to a boil in a 4-qt. pot. Add the asparagus and cook until just tender, about 3 minutes. Using a slotted spoon, transfer the asparagus to a bowl of ice water, reserving the boiling water. Let the asparagus chill for about 5 minutes, then drain and set aside.

**2.** Heat 2 tbsp. butter in a 10-inch skillet over medium-high heat. Add the mushrooms and cook, stirring occasionally, until just tender, about 6 minutes. Add the asparagus, season with salt and pepper, and remove the pan from heat; set aside.

**3.** Break the matzo into 1-inch pieces and transfer to a strainer set over the sink. Slowly pour the reserved boiling water over the matzo to soften it; let the matzo sit for 4 minutes.

**4.** Transfer the softened matzo to a bowl, add the eggs, and combine. Heat the remaining butter in a 10-inch skillet over medium-high heat. Add the matzo mixture, reduce the heat to medium-low, and cook, turning the mixture occasionally with a rubber spatula, until cooked to the desired doneness, about 4 minutes for soft curds. Divide the matzo mixture between 2 plates, top with the reserved mushrooms and asparagus, garnish with the parsley, and serve.

# Pasta and Noodles

We hunger for them like nearly nothing else: a plate of ethereal *tagliatelle alla bolognese*— ribbons of fresh, handmade egg pasta tossed with a long-simmered sauce of meat and tomatoes—or a deep bowl of Chinese noodles, stir-fried with pork and carrots. Pasta and noodles provide a canvas for a broad palette of ingredients, whether it's a lasagne filled with vegetables or good old American macaroni and cheese.

*A cook prepares tagliatelle egg noodles at La Vecchia Scuola Bolognese, a cooking school in Bologna, Italy.*

# Baked Ziti with Sausage

In Italian-American homes and red-sauce restaurants alike, this dish has remained a standby for generations. The ingredients are simple and the proportions generous, forming layer upon layer of pasta, beef *ragù*, creamy béchamel, and a beautifully browned topping of melted mozzarella and Parmigiano-Reggiano. This recipe calls for sweet Italian sausage to boost the flavor of the meaty filling, but it works well with spicy sausage, too.

¼   cup extra-virgin olive oil
1   lb. sweet Italian sausages, removed from casings and broken into ½-inch chunks
1   medium carrot, minced
1   medium onion, minced
1   rib celery, minced
1½  lbs. ground beef chuck
½   cup dry red wine
2   tbsp. tomato paste
1   28-oz. can whole peeled tomatoes, undrained and puréed
3   tbsp. minced flat-leaf parsley
    Kosher salt and freshly ground black pepper, to taste
5   tbsp. unsalted butter
5   tbsp. flour
2½  cups milk
¼   tsp. freshly grated nutmeg
1½  lbs. pasta, preferably ziti
2½  cups coarsely grated mozzarella cheese
½   cup freshly grated Parmigiano-Reggiano

*Serves 10*

1. To make the meat sauce: Heat the oil in a 6-qt. pot over medium-high heat. Add the sausage and cook, stirring occasionally, until well browned, 8–10 minutes. Using a slotted spoon, transfer the sausage to a plate and set aside. Add the carrots, onions, and celery and cook, stirring often, until soft and golden brown, about 15 minutes. Add the beef and cook, stirring and breaking it up with a wooden spoon, until browned, 8–10 minutes. Add the wine and cook, stirring, until evaporated, about 5 minutes. Add the tomato paste and cook, stirring frequently, for about 2 minutes. Add the tomato purée, reduce the heat to medium-low, and simmer, stirring occasionally, until the sauce is thick and the liquid has almost evaporated, about 1 hour. Stir in the reserved sausage and any juices from the plate, add the parsley, and season the sauce with salt and pepper. Remove from the heat and set the meat sauce aside.

2. Meanwhile, make the béchamel sauce: Melt 4 tbsp. butter in a 4-qt. saucepan over medium heat. Whisk in the flour and cook, whisking constantly, until it begins to bubble, about 2 minutes. While whisking, add the milk in a thin, steady stream. Bring the milk to a simmer and cook, whisking often, until the sauce thickens and coats the back of a spoon, 10–15 minutes. Remove the pan from the heat, add the nutmeg, season the béchamel sauce generously with salt and pepper, and set aside.

3. Heat the oven to 400°F. Bring a 6-qt. pot of salted water to a boil. Add the pasta and cook, stirring, until al dente, about 9 minutes. Drain the pasta, transfer to a bowl, stir in the reserved meat sauce, and season with salt and pepper. Grease a 4-qt. oval baking dish with the remaining butter and add half the pasta mixture. Pour half the béchamel over the pasta, spreading it evenly with a rubber spatula. Top the béchamel with the remaining pasta and then with the remaining béchamel. Sprinkle mozzarella and Parmigiano-Reggiano over the béchamel. Bake until golden brown and bubbly, about 25 minutes. Let the baked ziti sit for 10 minutes before serving.

## The Real Alfredo

How did fettuccine Alfredo become an American comfort-food staple? It all began in the early 1900s, when a Roman restaurateur named Alfredo di Lelio started serving a lavish version of *fettuccine al burro*, a homely dish of pasta tossed with nothing more than butter and Parmigiano-Reggiano. Di Lelio's signature dish was prepared tableside (as pictured below, in 1949); as the heat from the noodles melted the butter, the smiling and mustachioed di Lelio lifted and twirled the fettuccine with a gold fork and spoon, pausing to sprinkle in copious amounts of grated cheese. The dish and its creator became famous in Rome, but they were unknown outside of Italy until 1927, when George Rector, an American restaurant owner, writer, and bon vivant, sang their praises in his *Saturday Evening Post* column. Soon, celebrities like Mary Pickford and Douglas Fairbanks were seeking out the dish, followed by a steady stream of tourists. In 1966, food packagers jumped on the trend: the Pennsylvania Dutch noodle company started marketing fettuccine with a recipe for Alfredo's sauce, but it wasn't exactly authentic, considering that it called for cream and Swiss cheese.

# Fettuccine Alfredo

Mixing the ingredients on a warmed platter will help them melt quickly to make a satiny sauce. For the best results, use dried pasta, which doesn't break as easily during tossing as fresh egg pasta does.

| | |
|---|---|
| | Kosher salt, to taste |
| 1 | lb. dried fettuccine |
| 1 | cup (2 sticks) unsalted butter, cut into thin pats |
| 3¼ | cups finely grated Parmigiano-Reggiano |

*Serves 4*

**1.** Bring a large pot of salted water to a boil and add pasta; cook, stirring occasionally, until pasta is al dente, about 8 minutes. Meanwhile, place butter pats on a large, warmed serving platter. Drain pasta, reserving ¾ cup pasta water, and place the pasta over the butter on the platter Ⓐ.

**2.** Sprinkle Parmigiano-Reggiano evenly over pasta Ⓑ and drizzle with ¼ cup reserved pasta water. Using a large spoon and fork, gently toss the pasta with the butter and cheese, lifting and swirling the noodles and adding more pasta water as necessary to create a smooth sauce Ⓒ. Work in any melted butter and cheese that pools around the edges of the platter. Continue mixing pasta until the cheese and butter have fully melted and the noodles are coated, about 3 minutes. (For a quicker preparation, bring the reserved ¾ cup pasta water and the butter to a boil in a 12-inch skillet, and then add the pasta, sprinkle with the cheese, and toss with tongs over medium-low heat until the pasta is creamy and coated, about 2 minutes.)

**3.** Serve the fettuccine immediately on warmed plates Ⓓ.

# Orecchiette with Rapini and Goat Cheese

This dish is one of the best ways we know to use rapini (a k a broccoli rabe) when it's in season. Bright lemon zest, garlic, and red chile flakes play off the bitterness of the rapini and reveal its sweetness; soft, tangy goat cheese brings together the more piquant ingredients with the al dente pasta.

Kosher salt, to taste
1 bunch rapini (about 1 lb.), roughly chopped
⅓ cup extra-virgin olive oil
6 cloves garlic, crushed
¾ tsp. crushed red chile flakes
12 oz. orecchiette pasta
2 tbsp. lemon zest
4 oz. goat cheese, softened

*Serves 2–4*

1. Bring an 8-qt. pot of salted water to a boil. Add rapini and boil until crisp-tender, about 4 minutes. Using a slotted spoon, transfer rapini to a large bowl of ice water; chill. Drain rapini, pat dry, and set aside.

2. Heat oil in a 12-inch skillet over medium heat. Add garlic and cook, stirring occasionally, until golden, about 3 minutes. Add chile flakes and cook, stirring frequently, for 30 seconds. Add rapini, toss, and remove pan from heat; set aside.

3. Meanwhile, bring a 6-qt. pot of salted water to a boil. Add pasta and cook until al dente, about 10 minutes. Drain pasta and transfer pasta and lemon zest to reserved skillet over high heat. Toss to combine and season with salt. Divide pasta between bowls and add a dollop of goat cheese to each.

**COOKING NOTE** *Boiling a vegetable such as broccoli rabe and then submerging it, or "shocking" it, in an icy water bath is called blanching. The technique does three things: it preserves the vibrant color of the vegetable, transforms the vegetable's flavor ever so slightly, and arrests the cooking process, preserving the vegetable's crisp-tender texture.*

## Bright Green

Rapini is one of the most assertively flavored vegetables we've had the pleasure of tasting. Known in English as broccoli rabe, this member of the cabbage family (also referred to in Italian as *broccoletti di rape*, or "little turnip sprouts") only resembles broccoli in color and form, with its jagged leaves and slim stalks topped with green buds that blossom into yellow flowers. (Once rapini flowers, it becomes even more bitter.) Though the vegetable's origins are in Central Asia, where it's commonly stir-fried, it has also been embraced in the Italian kitchen, where cooks put its bright flavor to good use in side dishes, panini, and pastas. You'll often find rapini paired with garlic, which balances and takes the edge off the vegetable's pungent flavor. Blanching and shocking rapini in cold water before sautéing it is another way to temper its bitter edge.

## Simple Beauty

Cook butter long enough to see it sputter and foam, and something wonderful occurs. The color deepens to a golden brown, and the scent evolves from unctuous to toasty. This is brown butter, what the French call *beurre noisette* (literally, hazelnut butter), named both for its nutty color and flavor. It's also one of the simplest and most rewarding sauces a home cook can make.

When butter melts in a pan over heat, its butterfat separates from its milk solids and the water evaporates out, leaving behind a more concentrated, buttery liquid. The solids sink to the bottom of the pan and begin to caramelize, taking on an increasingly darker hue and richer flavor. A pale brown color will correspond to a faint nutty taste, while a deeper shade means a more profound flavor. (Don't let your brown butter get too dark, or the milk solids will scorch and the sauce will taste acrid and burnt.) It's important to remove brown butter from the pan as soon as caramelization is achieved; pour it into a small bowl so that the sauce doesn't continue cooking in the pan. Otherwise, you can stop the cooking process with the addition of something acidic; a squirt of lemon juice does the trick (while also balancing out the richness of the sauce). The addition of chopped parsley and lemon juice turns brown butter into the classic French sauce known as *beurre meuniere*, a traditional pairing for fish. Brown butter works well on its own, as a sauce for pasta or a garnish for fish or vegetables; it takes well to accompaniments like grated Parmigiano-Reggiano or Grana Padano, pine nuts, and spices like nutmeg and mace. Brown butter also brings a welcome depth of flavor to many baked goods, like pecan pie and shortbread.

# Brown Butter Pasta

Chef Gabrielle Hamilton of the New York City restaurant Prune shared this recipe for pasta, which she tosses in brown butter and pine nuts, and then tops with sunny-side-up eggs, Parmigiano-Reggiano, and nutmeg.

| | |
|---|---|
| | Kosher salt, to taste |
| 8 | oz. fresh pasta, such as fettuccine or tagliatelle (see recipe on page 86) |
| 1 | cup unsalted butter |
| ¾ | cup pine nuts |
| 4 | eggs |
| | Freshly ground black pepper, to taste |
| | Freshly grated Parmigiano-Reggiano and nutmeg, to taste |

*Serves 4*

**1.** Bring a large pot of salted water to a boil and add pasta; cook, stirring occasionally, until al dente, about 4 minutes. Set a strainer over a bowl; drain the pasta, reserving ½ cup pasta cooking water, and set aside.

**2.** Melt butter in a 12-inch skillet over medium heat. Add pine nuts and cook, stirring often, until golden brown, about 10 minutes. Using a slotted spoon, transfer pine nuts to a bowl. Working in two batches, crack eggs into butter and cook, spooning butter over yolks, until whites are set but yolks are still runny, about 3 minutes. Transfer eggs to a plate and keep warm. Add pasta and half the pine nuts to skillet and toss until hot. Stir in some of the reserved pasta water to create a sauce, and season with salt and pepper.

**3.** To serve, divide pasta between 4 serving plates and top each serving with a fried egg. Sprinkle pasta with remaining pine nuts, Parmigiano-Reggiano, and nutmeg.

# Vegetarian Lasagne

It's the archetypal family meal, a layering of sauce, cheese, and pasta that is uncomplicated and appealing. This lasagne is a vegetarian take on classic lasagne bolognese. Here, meat's savoriness is replaced with earthy shiitake mushrooms, and the noodles aren't boiled before baking, so they still retain some of their bite when they come out of the oven.

| | |
|---|---|
| 12 | tbsp. unsalted butter |
| 12 | sun-dried tomatoes |
| 1 | shallot, chopped |
| 1 | carrot, chopped |
| ½ | cup flour |
| 5 | cups milk |
| 1 | tsp. ground nutmeg |
| | Kosher salt and freshly ground black pepper, to taste |
| 3 | tbsp. extra-virgin olive oil |
| 2 | lbs. shiitake mushrooms, stemmed and quartered |
| ½ | lb. spinach, chopped |
| 6 | cloves garlic, chopped |
| 3 | tbsp. chopped flat-leaf parsley |
| 2 | tbsp. chopped oregano |
| 1 | tbsp. chopped rosemary |
| 1 | tbsp. chopped thyme |
| 1 | tbsp. tomato paste |
| 5 | cups whole canned tomatoes, crushed |
| 1 | lb. lasagna noodles |
| 2½ | cups grated Grana Padano or Parmigiano-Reggiano |
| 2½ | cups grated fontina |

*Serves 6–8*

**1.** Grease a deep 9 x 13-inch baking pan with 1 tbsp. butter; set aside. In a bowl, cover dried tomatoes with 1 cup boiling water; soak for about 20 minutes. Drain, chop, and set aside.

**2.** Make the béchamel sauce: Heat 8 tbsp. butter in a 4-qt. saucepan over medium heat. Add shallots and carrots and cook, stirring occasionally, until tender, about 5 minutes. Add the flour and cook, stirring, for 2 minutes. Whisk in milk and bring to a boil. Reduce heat to medium-low, bring to a simmer, and cook, whisking occasionally, until thick, about 25 minutes. Add nutmeg and season with salt and pepper.

**3.** Meanwhile, make the tomato sauce: Heat the olive oil and remaining butter in a 6-qt. pot over medium-high heat. Add the mushrooms; cook, stirring, until tender, about 10 minutes. Add the dried tomatoes, spinach, garlic, parsley, oregano, rosemary, thyme, and tomato paste and cook, stirring, for 3 minutes. Add the canned tomatoes and cook, stirring occasionally, until slightly thickened, about 10 minutes. Set the tomato sauce aside.

**4.** Heat the oven to 375°F. Spread 2 cups of the tomato sauce in the prepared baking dish. Cover with a layer of noodles. Spread 1 cup béchamel over top; sprinkle with ½ cup of each cheese and 2 cups tomato sauce. Repeat layering 2 more times. Top with the remaining noodles, tomato sauce, béchamel, and cheeses. Cover with aluminum foil, transfer to a baking sheet, and bake for 1 hour. Uncover and raise oven heat to 500°F. Bake until golden brown and bubbly, about 15 minutes. Cut into squares and serve.

## Italy's Other Ragù

The meaty wonder that is *ragù alla bolognese* may be the most famous pasta sauce in all of Italy, but other styles of *ragù* (which are sometimes called *sugo*) have similarly deep roots in other parts of the country. One of the most distinctive hails from Naples: *ragù alla napoletana* is a thick, robust tomato-based sauce cooked for hours with pork ribs, meatballs, fresh and cured sausages, and plenty of bones, which not only flavor the sauce but also lend it body. The thick sauce is tossed with hard durum wheat pasta of various shapes, from tubular *penne rigate* to spaghetti, and showered with grated cheese, often a pungent sheep's milk variety. There are countless other *ragù* in the southern part of Italy, including Sicilian and Calabrian versions made with meaty fish like tuna and swordfish. Unlike their counterparts in the north of Italy, virtually all southern *ragù* are heavy on tomatoes. In other parts of Italy, the type of meat is often the distinguishing characteristic of the sauce. In the province of Verona, for example, horse meat is a traditional ingredient, and Tuscans and Umbrians are partial to game, including duck, hare, and wild boar. Roman versions are often made with cured meats, and in Abruzzo and Molise, two provinces that sit adjacent to each other in the east-central part of the country, *ragù* of lamb and pork are the norm; they're often flavored with rosemary and served with pasta that's been cut with a tool with strings like a guitar called a *chitarra*, which creates rough edges to which the sauce clings beautifully.

# Pasta with Ragù
*Tagliatelle alla Ragù Bolognese*

This recipe for a hearty *ragù*, paired here with ribbons of tagliatelle pasta, came from Alessandra Spisni, who owns a cooking school in Bologna, Italy. Slow, low cooking thickens the sauce and marries the flavors of savory beef chuck and bright aromatics; making a double batch means that you can set aside some for use in a lasagne or another dish. Homemade pasta makes it all the more delicious; on the following pages, you'll find instructions on how to roll out, cut, and cook your own tagliatelle.

| | |
|---|---|
| ½ | cup butter |
| 3 | small yellow onions, minced |
| 2 | medium carrots, minced |
| 2 | ribs celery, minced |
| 2 | lbs. ground beef chuck |
| ½ | cup dry red wine |
| 2¾ | cups canned tomato purée |
| | Kosher salt and freshly ground black pepper, to taste |
| 2 | lbs. fresh tagliatelle or fettuccine |
| | Grated Parmigiano-Reggiano, for serving |

*Serves 8*

**1.** Heat the butter in a heavy-bottomed pot over medium heat. Add the onions, carrots, and celery and cook, stirring frequently, until vegetables are somewhat softened, about 8 minutes.

**2.** Raise the heat to medium-high, add the beef, and cook, stirring constantly, until the meat is broken up and just cooked through, about 7 minutes. Add the wine and cook, stirring occasionally, until evaporated, about 4 minutes. Stir in the tomato purée and 1½ cups water and bring to a boil over high heat.

**3.** Reduce the heat to low and simmer, partially covered, stirring occasionally, until the sauce is thick, about 2 hours. Season with salt and pepper.

**4.** Bring a 6-qt. pot of salted water to a boil. Add the pasta and cook, stirring, until al dente, or according to the package directions. Drain the pasta, transfer to a bowl, and toss with about half of the ragù, reserving the rest for another use. Serve warm with grated Parmigiano-Reggiano.

## Homemade Tagliatelle

Many Bolognese pasta makers roll their pasta dough by hand to make tagliatelle, but we found that using a hand-cranked pasta roller and cutting the dough with a knife yields excellent results.

Ⓐ On a clean surface, form 3 cups flour into a mound; create a well in center. Sprinkle 1 tsp. kosher salt over flour. Add 3 eggs, 1 egg yolk, 2 tbsp. water, and 1 tbsp. olive oil to well.

Ⓑ Using a fork, incorporate eggs and liquid in a circular motion, pulling in small amounts of flour until dough becomes stiff.

Ⓒ Knead dough, adding a little flour as necessary, until it's smooth and elastic, about 10 minutes. Wrap in plastic wrap; let rest for 30 minutes.

Ⓓ Cut dough into quarters.

Ⓔ Flatten 1 quarter into a rectangle (cover others with a towel). Pass dough through a hand-cranked pasta roller set at widest setting.

Ⓕ Fold dough in thirds, creating another rectangle; feed open edge through roller set at widest setting. Fold again; roll twice more using same setting. Decrease setting one notch and roll the pasta through again; repeat, decreasing setting each time until you've reached the second-to-last setting, creating a ¹⁄₁₆-inch thick sheet.

Ⓖ Sprinkle sheet with flour; halve crosswise. Transfer to flour-dusted parchment paper. Repeat with the remaining dough, adding flour-dusted parchment paper between each layer.

Ⓗ Tightly roll each sheet, from short end to short end; cut cylinder crosswise into ³⁄₈-inch wide strips. Unroll strips and toss with flour; spread on a floured parchment sheet. Let dry for 30 minutes. To serve: Cook tagliatelle in salted boiling water until al dente, about 3–4 minutes. Drain; transfer to a bowl and toss with 2 cups *ragù* (or more, to taste); see recipe on page 84. Serve with grated Parmigiano-Reggiano.

*Serves 4*

Ⓐ

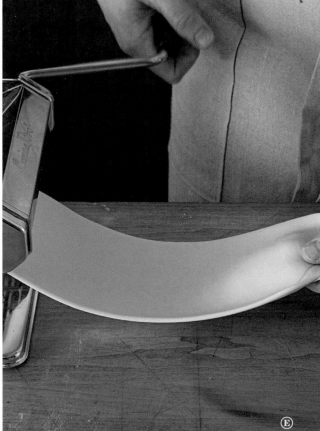

Ⓔ

# Bucatini with Spicy Tomato Sauce

*Bucatini all'Amatriciana*

This Roman classic is flavored with *guanciale,* or cured pork jowl, though pancetta is a fine substitute. Toasting the black pepper in the fat rendered out from the *guanciale* boosts the flavor of this sauce.

| | |
|---|---|
| 3 | tbsp. extra-virgin olive oil |
| 4 | oz. thinly sliced guanciale or pancetta, cut into ¾-inch pieces |
| | Freshly cracked black pepper, to taste |
| 2 | cloves garlic, minced |
| 1 | small carrot, minced |
| ½ | medium onion, minced |
| ½ | tsp. crushed red chile flakes |
| 1 | 28-oz. can peeled tomatoes, preferably San Marzano, undrained and puréed |
| | Kosher salt, to taste |
| 1 | lb. bucatini or spaghetti |
| 1¼ | cups grated Pecorino Romano |

*Serves 4*

**1.** Heat oil in a large, high-sided skillet over medium heat. Add guanciale; cook, stirring, until lightly browned, 6–8 minutes. Add pepper; cook, stirring often, until toasted and fragrant, about 2 minutes more. Increase heat to medium-high; add garlic, carrots, and onions and cook, stirring occasionally, until soft, about 6 minutes. Add chile flakes; cook for 1 minute. Stir in tomato purée, reduce heat to medium-low, and simmer, stirring occasionally, until sauce thickens and flavors meld, 20–25 minutes. Season with salt; keep warm.

**2.** Bring a 6-qt. pot of salted water to a boil. Add pasta and cook until just al dente, 6–8 minutes. Reserve ½ cup pasta water; drain pasta. Heat reserved sauce over medium heat. Add pasta and reserved water; cook, tossing, until sauce clings to pasta, 2–3 minutes. Add ½ cup Pecorino Romano; toss. Divide between serving bowls; serve with remaining Pecorino Romano.

## Secret Ingredient

Cured pork jowl, known as *guanciale*, is an essential component of many Roman pasta dishes, including *spaghetti alla carbonara* and *bucatini all'amatriciana*. But it can also be sautéed with vegetables, added to stewed fava beans, or cooked with meat or fish so that its fragrant fat renders out and suffuses the dish. Usually sold whole, *guanciale* has a flavor that is less salty but stronger and fattier than its cousin pancetta—Italian salt-cured pork belly—and a texture that's somewhat softer. While *guanciale*, which can be cured with everything from black pepper to spices, is traditionally unsmoked, smoked versions are popular nowadays in Rome. Smoked *guanciale* isn't readily available in the United States, but Mauro Trabalza, the chef at Sora Lella, a restaurant in Rome that has an outpost in New York City, recommends a mixture of three parts regular *guanciale* or pancetta to one part bacon to approximate the flavor of smoked *guanciale*.

# Macaroni and Cheese with Ham

You can use any kind of cooked or cured ham for this luscious mac and cheese, which has a pleasingly tangy edge thanks to the addition of a little blue cheese. Black Forest ham, for example, will add a note of subtle sweetness, while country ham will provide an earthy, deeply savory flavor and a slightly chewy texture.

| | |
|---|---|
| 11 | tbsp. unsalted butter, melted |
| | Kosher salt, to taste |
| 12 | oz. pasta, such as rigatoni |
| 2 | slices crustless white bread |
| 2 | tsp. minced fresh thyme |
| 1 | small onion, minced |
| ½ | cup flour |
| 3 | cups milk |
| 2 | cups heavy cream |
| 12 | oz. grated sharp cheddar cheese |
| 8 | oz. cooked ham (any variety will do), roughly chopped |
| 3 | oz. blue cheese, crumbled |
| ½ | cup minced flat-leaf parsley |
| ¼ | tsp. hot sauce, such as Tabasco |
| 4 | scallions, minced |
| ¼ | tsp. freshly ground black pepper |
| ⅛ | tsp. freshly ground nutmeg |

*Serves 8–10*

**1.** Grease a 2-qt. baking dish with 1 tbsp. melted butter and set aside. Bring a 6-qt. pot of salted water to a boil, add the pasta, and cook until al dente, about 8 minutes. Drain the pasta, rinse, and set aside. Pulse the bread in a food processor until finely ground, mix with 4 tbsp. butter, and set aside.

**2.** Heat the oven to 400°F. Melt the remaining butter in a 6-qt. pot over medium heat. Add the thyme and onions and cook until soft, about 6 minutes. Whisk in the flour and cook for about 3 minutes. Whisk in the milk and cream. Increase the heat to medium-high and cook, whisking, until thick, 10–12 minutes. Whisk in the cheddar, ham, blue cheese, parsley, hot sauce, scallions, pepper, and nutmeg. Taste and season with salt as needed. Stir in the pasta, transfer to the prepared baking dish, and sprinkle with the bread crumbs. Bake until golden brown and bubbly, 30–40 minutes.

**COOKING NOTE** *There are a few tried-and-true secrets to making macaroni and cheese with the perfect creamy texture. You need a smooth sauce as a base—in this case, it's a velvety béchamel made of butter, flour, milk, and cream. And you need to make sure the cheese melts evenly and becomes one with that sauce. Firm cheeses like cheddar, Comté, fontina, and Gruyère are reliable choices. Let the cheese come to room temperature before you use it, shred it as finely as possible, and heat it gently with the sauce; a blast of high heat can cause proteins in the cheese to separate from the fats, resulting in a macaroni and cheese that's both grainy and oily.*

*A volunteer plates spaghetti with homemade tomato sauce at the Sacred Heart Church in Cincinnati, Ohio. The church has been hosting its biannual Italian Spaghetti and Ravioli Dinner since 1910.*

# Figaretti's "Godfather II" Linguine

This dish, a mainstay at Figaretti's restaurant in Wheeling, West Virginia, is Italian-American cooking at its bighearted, bountiful best: shrimp and mussels, peppers and tomatoes, fresh basil, white wine, and silky linguine.

Kosher salt, to taste
8 oz. dried linguine
½ cup extra-virgin olive oil
½ cup chopped green bell pepper
½ cup chopped red bell pepper
3 cloves garlic, minced
1 small yellow onion, chopped
⅓ cup white wine
8 mussels, scrubbed and debearded
½ cup halved cherry tomatoes
2 tbsp. unsalted butter
8 large shrimp, peeled and deveined
8 leaves basil, torn, plus more for garnish
Freshly ground black pepper, to taste
½ cup grated Asiago cheese
4 lemon wedges

*Serves 2*

**1.** Bring a pot of salted water to a boil over high heat. Add the linguine; cook until al dente, 8–10 minutes. Drain the pasta; reserve ¼ cup pasta water.

**2.** Meanwhile, heat the olive oil in a 12-inch skillet over medium-high heat. Add the green and red peppers, garlic, and onion; cook until they begin to soften, about 3 minutes. Add the wine and the mussels; cook, covered, until the mussels open, about 2 minutes. Add reserved pasta water, tomatoes, butter, and shrimp and cook, stirring, until the shrimp are just pink, about 1 minute. Add the cooked linguine, toss to combine, and cook, stirring occasionally, until the sauce thickens and clings to the pasta. Stir in the basil and season with salt and pepper.

**3.** Divide pasta between 2 bowls. Sprinkle with more basil and Asiago and garnish with lemon wedges.

## America's First Food Critic

I first learned about the great Italian-American fare at Figaretti's in West Virginia by reading an old guidebook written by Duncan Hines. Today, Duncan Hines is invariably associated with the boxed cake mixes that bear his name, but before he started hawking mass-produced food products in the 1950s, he reigned as one of the country's most influential restaurant critics. In the days before Zagat Surveys, the words "Recommended by Duncan Hines" were a seal of approval proudly displayed outside restaurants across the country. Duncan Hines was born in Bowling Green, Kentucky, in 1880. He first got the idea of reviewing restaurants for travelers when he was working as a salesman for printing businesses; driving around the country to meet with clients, he filled a notebook with thoughts about his favorite places to eat along the way. Hines published the first *Adventures in Good Eating* guide in 1936. The guide was a best-seller and was updated every year until 1962. In 1949, Hines launched a line of products on the strength of his steadfast reputation; ice cream came first, followed by the popular cake mixes. Today, I continue to take inspiration from his simple mission: to introduce travelers to "the refinements of good living, while seeing America." —*Todd Coleman*

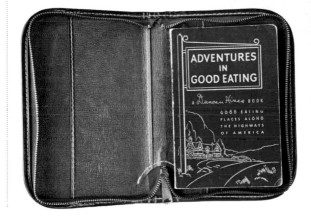

## Nice Slices

Uniformly sliced vegetables are essential to stir-fries, so that the ingredients will cook evenly. To transform carrots into the thin sticks called julienne requires patient slicing. Most professional cooks chop their carrots into 2-inch-long segments, square off and discard the edges, and

cut the segments into thin planks, which they then stack up and slice into slivers. It's a perfectly serviceable way of going about it, but it produces a lot of wasted carrot. We prefer the following technique, which we learned from Shirley Cheng, a professor of Asian cooking at the Culinary Institute of America in Hyde Park, New York. Here's how to do it.

Ⓐ Trim and peel a carrot. Using a large, sharp knife, slice on a deep diagonal into thin, broad slices, keeping the overlapping slices nestled close together as you work. Cutting on the diagonal allows you to use almost the whole carrot; slices from the tapered end will be about the same length as those from the thicker end.

Ⓑ Spread the carrot slices out like a deck of cards, so that one slice overlaps most of another.

Ⓒ Working from one end of the pile to the other, cut the carrot slices into thin slivers, holding the carrots down firmly with your free hand as you go.

# Everyday Fried Noodles
*Tian Tian Chao Mian*

In this Beijing-style noodle stir-fry, ingredients go into the wok in a measured progression so that each one cooks to the point of optimal flavor and texture. Carrots and onions are stir-fried just long enough to reveal their sweetness; pork, ginger, and garlic release their fragrance into the hot oil; then soy sauce, rice wine, and sugar cook down quickly into a sauce that clings to the noodles, which get a final toss in the wok along with salted cucumber and a drizzle of sesame oil. The subtle, surprising result is a beautiful testament to what a little care applied to a few simple elements can produce.

| | |
|---|---|
| ½ | small seedless cucumber, peeled and julienned |
| | Kosher salt, to taste |
| 3 | tbsp. canola oil |
| 1 | medium carrot, julienned |
| 1 | medium onion, thinly sliced |
| ¼ | lb. ground pork |
| 4 | cloves garlic, minced |
| 1 | 1-inch piece ginger, minced |
| 6 | scallions, minced |
| 1½ | tbsp. dark soy sauce |
| 1½ | tbsp. rice cooking wine |
| 1½ | tsp. sugar |
| 2 | cups bean sprouts |
| 6 | oz. dried flat noodles, boiled and rinsed under cold water |
| 1 | tbsp. Asian sesame oil |

*Serves 2–4*

**1.** Toss the cucumbers and a pinch of salt together in a small bowl; set aside for at least 5 minutes. Heat a 14-inch wok (or a stainless-steel skillet) over high heat until it begins to smoke. Add 1 tbsp. oil around the edge of the wok and swirl to coat the bottom and sides of the wok. Add the carrots and onions and cook until softened, about 1 minute. Transfer to a plate and set aside.

**2.** Return the wok to high heat and add the remaining oil. Add the pork, garlic, ginger, and half of the scallions and cook, breaking the pork into small pieces, until browned, 3–4 minutes.

**3.** Add the soy sauce, rice cooking wine, sugar, bean sprouts, and reserved carrots and onions. Cook, stirring, until hot, 30 seconds.

**4.** Add the reserved cucumbers, remaining scallions, noodles, and sesame oil and cook, tossing, until hot, about 1 minute. Season with salt. Divide between plates and serve hot.

# Fish and Shellfish

Fish markets are some of the most extraordinary places on the planet: from the sprawling wholesale marts of Bangkok or New York City to the dockside stalls in coastal villages around the world. It's not just the sensory experience—the ocean scent, the glistening fish—that we find alluring; it's the promise of a great meal. Stuffed clams, crisp-fried catfish, spicy Veracruz-style snapper—these dishes make the most of the ocean's bounty and reaffirm our love of the sea, no matter how far from it we happen to be.

*A fisherman delivers his daily catch to a waterfront fish market on the coast of Tanzania.*

# New Orleans–Style BBQ Shrimp

Despite the name, these shrimp are cooked in a skillet, not on a grill; "barbecue," in this case, refers to the sweet-hot sauce served with them. Tory McPhail, the chef at the legendary New Orleans restaurant Commander's Palace, serves this house specialty with plenty of crusty bread for mopping up that mouthwatering sauce.

| | |
|---|---|
| 16 | jumbo shrimp, peeled and deveined, tails left on |
| 2 | tbsp. Creole or Cajun seasoning, such as Tony Chachere's brand |
| ¼ | cup canola oil |
| 4 | cloves garlic, minced |
| 2 | tbsp. minced fresh rosemary leaves |
| ½ | cup beer, preferably Abita Amber |
| 6 | tbsp. hot sauce |
| 6 | tbsp. Worcestershire |
| 5 | tbsp. fresh lemon juice |
| 12 | tbsp. unsalted cold butter, cut into small pieces |
| 1 | loaf crusty French bread, for serving |

*Serves 4*

**1.** Put the shrimp and Creole seasoning into a bowl and toss to coat; set aside.

**2.** Heat a large skillet over medium heat until hot. Add the oil and garlic to the skillet and cook until the garlic is golden, about 1 minute. Add the rosemary and cook for 2–3 seconds. Add the shrimp and cook, flipping once, until they start to turn pink, about 30 seconds. Transfer the shrimp to a large plate and set aside. Add the beer, hot sauce, Worcestershire, and lemon juice to the skillet and stir well. Cook, stirring, until thickened, 7–8 minutes.

**3.** Remove the skillet from the heat and whisk in the butter, a few pieces at a time (the sauce will start to thicken). Return the shrimp to the skillet and toss to coat. Return the skillet to medium heat and cook until the shrimp are cooked through, 2–3 minutes. Transfer the shrimp and sauce to 4 plates. Serve with chunks of crusty bread.

## Let the Good Times Roll

There's no place I'd rather be on a Sunday morning than Commander's Palace in New Orleans' Garden District, with a milk punch in hand and a plate of eggs Sardou, BBQ shrimp, or redfish Lyonnaise on the way. A brass band ambles from room to room, silverware clanks, conversation bubbles forth. In the foyer, Ella Brennan, the matriarch of the family that has run this restaurant for the past four decades, is holding court and telling stories. Her niece, Lally, escorts guests to the bar—which happens to be in the kitchen. No one does restaurants like the Brennans, and no restaurant in that family's expanding empire, which includes a dozen or so bistros, steak houses, and cafés in New Orleans and other cities across the South, is a more exuberant example of the manifold glories of dining in the Crescent City than Commander's Palace. It is formal, but good fun. The fare is traditional—a marriage of elegant, European-inflected Creole dishes with more rustic Cajun ones—with just enough whimsy to keep it interesting. With flaming tableside desserts like bananas Foster (a dish Miss Ella invented on the fly one night back in the 1960s at the family's restaurant, Brennan's), Commander's distinguishes itself from other temples of New Orleans gastronomy by embracing the city's joie de vivre. —*Dana Bowen*

## Clam Varieties

With their sweet, briny flavor, clams are at the heart of some of New England's best cooking. The most common species in the United States belong to the hardshell variety, which is native to the Eastern seaboard; its classification, *Mercenaria mercenaria*, derives from the Latin word for money, and refers to the clam shells  Native Americans used to polish into beads for wampum. At one time, the names for different clams reflected a place of origin—littlenecks ① came from Little Neck, Long Island; cherry-stones ②  came from Cherrystone Creek in Virginia. But nowadays, hardshell clams' names distinguish size, not origin. The East Coast is arguably home to the country's most fervent clam culture, from the smallest to the largest: there are countnecks (1–1½ inches), littlenecks (1½–2 inches), top-

 necks (2–2½ inches), cherrystones (2½–3 inches), and quahogs (3 inches or more ④).

Usually, the smaller the hard clam, the more it costs, since its meat is tenderer and delicately flavored, and ideal for eating raw. Larger quahogs or "chowdah" clams, as they're called in New England, are firmer and more emphatically flavored; they're often chopped and then simmered, stewed, fried, or used for stuffing. Delicate softshell clams ③ or steamers—or as the old-timers say, pissers— are another species entirely (*Mya arenaria*). These clams, with their fragile shells and a necklike siphon, are always cooked. Traditionalists steam them in their shells in a couple of inches of seawater, or shuck them for that quintessential summer specialty, fried clams.

# Stuffies

They've got a way with shellfish in Rhode Island, a state that surely has more roadside clam shacks per capita than any other. An all-time Ocean State favorite is stuffed quahogs—the biggest of the Atlantic hardshell clams—affectionately known as stuffies. The garlicky *linguiça* sausage in the stuffing is a legacy of Rhode Island's Portuguese immigrants. (Pictured at right, a Rhode Island clam fisherman in the 1940s.)

| | |
|---|---|
| 15 | slices white sandwich bread |
| 3 | tbsp. extra-virgin olive oil |
| ¾ | lb. linguiça (Portuguese sausage), minced |
| 6 | cloves garlic, minced |
| 2 | ribs celery, minced |
| 1 | small yellow onion, minced |
| 1 | small green bell pepper, cored, seeded, and minced |
| 2¼ | cups chopped clam meat, preferably quahogs |
| ¾ | cup clam juice or strained clam liquor |
| 6 | tbsp. minced flat-leaf parsley |
| 3 | tbsp. fresh lemon juice |
| 1½ | tbsp. Tabasco |
| 1½ | tbsp. Worcestershire |
| 6 | tbsp. unsalted butter, cubed |
| | Kosher salt and freshly ground black pepper, to taste |
| 16 | empty large quahog half shells |
| | Paprika, to taste |
| | Lemon wedges, for serving |

*Serves 6–8*

**1.** Heat the oven to 275°F. Pulse the bread in a food processor into fine crumbs. Transfer to a baking sheet and bake, tossing often, until dried, 15–20 minutes; set aside.

**2.** Raise the oven heat to 425°F. Heat the oil in a large skillet over medium heat. Add the sausage, garlic, celery, onions, and peppers and cook until soft, 12–15 minutes. Add the clams, clam juice, parsley, lemon juice, Tabasco, and Worcestershire and bring to a boil. Reduce the heat to medium-low and add the butter. Add the bread crumbs and salt and pepper; stir.

**3.** Divide the stuffing between the shells and place on a baking sheet. Bake until browned, about 25 minutes. Sprinkle with paprika and serve with lemon wedges.

# Veracruz-Style Red Snapper

*Pescado a la Veracruzana*

The Caribbean-inflected cuisine of the coastal city of Veracruz, in southeastern Mexico, is one of bright flavors and abundant seafood; ingredients like capers and olives are a legacy of the Spanish, who imported products from Europe into Mexico via this port throughout the colonial period. Cooks in Veracruz often bake fish filets together with a sauce of tomatoes, capers, olives, and jalapeños. We've found that searing the fish separately preserves its firm texture, and the same skillet can then be used to make a quick and flavorful pan sauce.

4   6- to 8-oz. skin-on boneless
    filets of red snapper,
    striped bass, or redfish
    Kosher salt and freshly
    ground black pepper,
    to taste
½   cup flour
6   tbsp. extra-virgin olive oil
1   small white onion, minced
2   pickled jalapeños, minced
3   tbsp. liquid from a jar
    of pickled jalapeños
2   tbsp. salt-packed
    capers, soaked, drained,
    and minced
½   tsp. dried oregano
6   cloves garlic, minced
2   bay leaves
¼   cup fish or chicken stock
¼   cup fresh lime juice
8   large green olives, such
    as manzanitas, pitted and
    roughly chopped
3   large tomatoes, peeled,
    seeded, and chopped
    (or one 28-oz. can whole
    peeled tomatoes, drained
    and chopped)
2   tbsp. roughly chopped
    flat-leaf parsley
2   tbsp. roughly chopped
    fresh cilantro

*Serves 4*

**1.** Heat the oven to 200°F. Season the snapper filets with salt and pepper. Put the flour on a plate and dredge the fish in the flour, shaking off the excess. Heat 2 tbsp. oil in a 12-inch nonstick skillet over medium-high heat. Add 2 fish filets and cook, pressing down with a spatula (to prevent the filet from curling up) and flipping once, until golden brown, about 4 minutes. Transfer the fish to a baking sheet and repeat with 2 more tbsp. oil and the remaining fish filets. Transfer baking sheet to the oven to keep fish warm.

**2.** Return the skillet to medium-high heat with the remaining oil. Add the onions and cook, stirring occasionally, until soft, about 10 minutes. Add the pickled jalapeños, jalapeño liquid, capers, oregano, garlic, and bay leaves and cook, stirring occasionally, until the garlic is soft, about 3 minutes. Add the stock, lime-juice, olives, tomatoes, parsley, and cilantro and cook, stirring occasionally, until the flavors meld, about 5 minutes. Season the sauce with salt and pepper. Transfer the fish to a platter, spoon the sauce over the fish, and serve.

Each summer, they rush upriver with remarkable urgency—schools of indomitable salmon, leaping skyward in glistening arcs of silver as they return from the ocean depths to their freshwater birthplaces to spawn. For centuries, North American fishermen and cooks have eagerly awaited this annual spring pilgrimage; it signals a return to a season of abundance and vitality in the kitchen. Different waterways along North America's West Coast attract different species of Pacific salmon (see "Know Your Salmon," page 108): Alaska's Yukon River, for example, is known for king salmon, while Washington's Puget Sound yields mostly pink and sockeye salmon. On the Atlantic, however, wild salmon populations are less than half of what they were only 20 years ago; just a few countries in the North Atlantic, including Ireland and Iceland, still support a very small salmon fishery.

# Broiled Salmon Steaks with Tomatoes, Onions, and Tarragon

Meaty salmon steaks take well to broiling with sweet roasted vegetables and herbs.

½ cup plus 4 tbsp. extra-virgin olive oil
2 large yellow onions
4 medium tomatoes
16 cloves garlic, smashed
10 sprigs each of fresh thyme and oregano, plus ½ tbsp. each of fresh thyme and fresh oregano leaves, roughly chopped
Kosher salt and freshly ground black pepper, to taste
4 10-oz. bone-in salmon steaks
4 thin slices of lemon
2 tbsp. fresh tarragon leaves
2 tbsp. Pernod

*Serves 4*

**1.** Heat oven to 450°F. Line a baking sheet with aluminum foil and grease it with ¼ cup extra-virgin olive oil.

**2.** Cut onions into ¼-inch-thick rings; cut tomatoes into ½-inch slices. Spread out the onions and tomatoes on the baking sheet to form a bed for the salmon steaks. Tuck garlic, thyme, and oregano between vegetables and drizzle with ¼ cup olive oil. Season the vegetables with kosher salt and freshly ground black pepper to taste. Roast the vegetables until soft and lightly browned, about 25 minutes.

**3.** Remove the baking sheet from the oven. Set an oven rack 3 inches from the broiler element; heat oven to broil. Arrange salmon steaks on top of the roasted vegetables and drizzle with 2 tbsp. oil, and season with freshly ground black pepper to taste. Place 1 slice of lemon on each salmon steak and sprinkle ½ tbsp. chopped thyme and ½ tbsp. chopped oregano over the fish. Broil salmon until lightly browned and just cooked through, about 5 minutes.

**4.** To serve, transfer salmon and vegetables to a platter. Sprinkle with tarragon, Pernod, and remaining oil.

## Know Your Salmon

Different varieties of salmon vary substantially in taste and texture, but they all share one cardinal trait: a high fat content, which gives their flesh a rich flavor and lush texture. All wild salmon taste their best when caught just before their journey home to freshwater spawning grounds, since they prepare for the trip by fattening up on ocean crustaceans. Featured here are the six varieties available in the United States. Also known as chinook salmon, the mighty **king** ① can weigh well over a hundred pounds; its habitat ranges from California to Alaska. The meaty fish has a pure flavor and ample fat and cooks beautifully over a charcoal fire. The **coho salmon** ②, also called silver salmon, constitutes just 10 percent of the commercial salmon fishery in the United States. Making its home in the waters from Oregon to Alaska and available in markets from late summer through fall, the fish has a firm texture and a rich, gamy flavor suited to simple preparations like poaching. **Pink salmon** ③, also called humpback salmon, is the smallest variety available in this country, averaging only five pounds; the most abundant of our salmons, it's often canned. Lower in fat, its delicate, sweet flesh has a subtle flavor best brought out by pan-frying or whole-roasting. Sometimes known as leaper salmon, the **Atlantic salmon** ④ once flourished in North Atlantic waters, but overfishing, pollution, and a host of other factors have decimated wild stocks. Demand for this fatty, full-flavored salmon, probably the most versatile variety when it comes to cooking, is met mostly by fish farms, which now produce more than half of all the salmon sold in this country. The flesh of the red salmon, or **sockeye, salmon** ⑤, a variety of Pacific salmon whose range stretches from British Columbia to Alaska and which is the second-fattiest type, has a distinctive, deep orange-red color and is dense and full-flavored. Sockeye, which first comes to market in May, is usually the variety favored for raw preparations. The abundant and relatively neutral-tasting **chum salmon** ⑥, sometimes called keta salmon, is second only to the king in size and inhabits waters throughout the Pacific Northwest; chum salmon is harvested in the late fall and is most often canned, smoked, or cured.

# Deep-Fried Southern Catfish

Melt-in-your-mouth fried catfish is a veritable birthright if you're from the Deep South, where family-style restaurants called catfish houses are fixtures of the rural landscape. This dish doesn't call for any dressing up, aside from a big spoonful of tangy tartar sauce and an ice-cold beer.

|   | |
|---|---|
|   | Canola or peanut oil, for frying |
| 2 | cups yellow cornmeal |
| 1⅓ | cups flour |
| ¼ | cup seasoned salt, such as Lawry's |
| 2 | tbsp. baking powder |
| 1 | tbsp. freshly ground black pepper |
| 4 | 3- to 5-oz. boneless, skinless catfish filets or bone-in, skinless catfish steaks |
| ½ | lemon, cut into wedges, for serving |
|   | Tartar sauce, for serving |

*Serves 2*

**1.** Pour oil into an 8-qt. pot to a depth of 3 inches and heat over medium-high heat until a deep-fry thermometer reads 350°F.

**2.** Meanwhile, combine the cornmeal, flour, seasoned salt, baking powder, and pepper in a large bowl. Add the catfish and toss to coat. Gently shake off the excess cornmeal mixture and transfer the catfish to a wire rack set over a rimmed baking sheet.

**3.** Working in 2 batches, fry the catfish in the hot oil until golden brown and cooked through, about 6 minutes. Using tongs, transfer the catfish to a wire cooling rack set over a rimmed baking sheet to drain. Transfer the fish to 2 plates and serve with a lemon wedge and tartar sauce.

## Pride of the Delta

On a Saturday night in Mississippi, there's always a wait at the local catfish houses, those family-style fried-fish restaurants that serve cornmeal-dusted filets piled on a plate with lemon wedges, tartar sauce, and a mound of fries and hush puppies. "Catfish is to Mississippi what crawfish is to Louisiana," says Brandon Hughes, a fry cook at Taylor Grocery, a popular catfish house in Oxford, Mississippi. There are 28 North American species of catfish (so named because of its whiskers, or barbels, which the fish uses to search for food), and many others that are native to parts of Asia, where catfish is also prized, but it is *Ictalurus punctatus*, commonly called channel catfish, that is favored across the American South. The fish fried at places like Taylor's and Carmack aren't wild: they are sustainably farmed in the Mississippi Delta. Catfish may be the world's only widely consumed fish that tastes better farmed than wild. Wild catfish feed on the pond bed, which gives them a muddy flavor, but farm-raised fish have a sweet, clean, and nutty taste that lends itself to even more than frying; it's also a perfect canvas for everything from rémoulade-smothered po'boys to fiery curries. Catfish has long been considered a trash fish, a misconception that a single bite of farmed catfish will instantly erase. "The catfish," wrote Mark Twain, "is good enough fish for anybody." You don't have to tell that to the folks in Mississippi, where catfish is king.
—*Hunter Lewis*

# Cod Cakes with Chowchow

These pan-fried cod cakes, served with a tart-sweet relish of pickled vegetables called chowchow, come from Eva Murphy, a home cook in Cape Breton Island, off Nova Scotia, who also shared her corn chowder recipe (see page 44). The dish makes good use of the firm-fleshed cod caught nearby.

### FOR THE CHOWCHOW:

- 1½ lbs. unripe green tomatoes, cored and minced
- 1 yellow onion, minced
- 1 rib celery, minced
- ½ medium green bell pepper, cored, seeded, and minced
- ½ medium red bell pepper, cored, seeded, and minced
- 2 tbsp. kosher salt
- ½ cup sugar
- ⅓ cup distilled white vinegar
- 1½ tsp. dry mustard
- 1½ tsp. yellow mustard seeds
- 1 tsp. celery seeds
- 1 tsp. crushed chile flakes
- ¼ tsp. ground coriander

### FOR THE COD CAKES:

- 6 tbsp. extra-virgin olive oil
- 2 ribs celery, minced
- 1 medium onion, minced
- 1 clove garlic, minced
- 2 russet potatoes (about 1 lb.), peeled and cut into ¼-inch cubes
  Kosher salt, to taste
- 1 lb. boneless, skinless cod filets
  Freshly ground black pepper, to taste
- ½ cup dried bread crumbs
- ¼ cup mayonnaise
- 2 tbsp. minced fresh dill
- 2 tbsp. minced parsley
- 1 egg yolk, beaten
- 1 tbsp. fresh lemon juice
- 4 tbsp. unsalted butter

*Serves 4*

1. Make the chowchow: Toss the tomatoes, onions, celery, and peppers in a large bowl with the salt. Cover with plastic wrap and let sit at room temperature for 4 hours or overnight. Transfer the vegetables to a sieve and press to extract the excess juices; discard the juices.

2. Transfer the vegetables to a 6-qt. saucepan and add the remaining ingredients. Cover, bring the mixture to a boil, reduce heat to medium-low, and simmer, stirring occasionally, until the vegetables are very soft, about 2½ hours. Transfer the relish to a jar and let cool. Cover and refrigerate for up to 2 weeks.

3. Make the cod cakes: Heat 2 tbsp. oil in a 12-inch skillet over medium heat. Add the celery, onions, and garlic and cook, stirring occasionally, until soft, about 8 minutes. Transfer the celery–onion mixture to a large bowl and set aside.

4. Put the potatoes into a 4-qt. pot, cover with salted water by 1 inch, and bring to a boil. Reduce the heat to medium and simmer until the potatoes are tender, about 15 minutes. Drain; transfer half the potatoes to a plate and set aside to let cool. Transfer the remaining potatoes to a bowl and mash with a fork. Transfer the mashed potatoes to the reserved bowl of celery–onion mixture and set aside to cool.

5. Season the cod with salt and pepper. Heat 2 tbsp. oil in a 12-inch nonstick skillet over medium heat. Add the cod and cook, turning once with a metal spatula, until cooked through, about 8 minutes. Transfer the cod filets to a plate and let cool. Break the cod into 1-inch chunks and set aside.

6. Add the bread crumbs, mayonnaise, herbs, egg yolk, and lemon juice to the potato–onion mixture and stir vigorously to combine. Add the reserved cubed potatoes and the cod and mix gently to combine. Using your hands, divide the mixture into 8 equal portions and form into cakes approximately 3 inches in diameter. Transfer the cakes to a wax paper–lined baking sheet, cover with plastic wrap, and refrigerate for 30 minutes until firm.

7. Working in 2 batches, heat remaining oil and butter in the skillet over medium-high heat. Add the cod cakes and cook, flipping once, until golden brown, about 8 minutes. Transfer cakes to a platter. Serve with chowchow and lemon halves, if you like.

# Grilled Lobster with Cilantro–Chile Butter

Halving and grilling is an excellent way to cook a whole lobster; the tender meat cooks inside the cupped shell along with melted butter. In this variation on that theme, the crustacean is seasoned with cilantro, chiles, and lime zest.

| | |
|---|---|
| 4 | oz. unsalted butter, softened |
| 3 | tbsp. minced cilantro |
| 4 | Fresno or Holland chiles, stemmed, seeded, and minced |
| 1 | lime, zested and quartered |
| 2 | 2-lb. live lobsters |
| ¼ | cup extra-virgin olive oil Kosher salt and freshly ground black pepper, to taste |

*Serves 2–4*

**1.** In a small bowl, stir together the butter, cilantro, chiles, and lime zest; set aside. Using a heavy cleaver, split each lobster in half lengthwise through its head and its tail. Scoop out and discard the gravel sac near the head and the vein running along the back. Twist off the lobster claws. Transfer the lobster halves, flesh side up, to a baking sheet; crack the lobster claws and transfer them to the baking sheet. Drizzle the lobster halves and claws with oil and season them with salt and pepper.

**2.** Build a medium-hot fire in a charcoal grill or heat a gas grill to medium-high. (Alternatively, heat a 12-inch cast-iron grill pan over medium-high heat.) Place lobster halves (flesh side down) and claws on grill and cook for 5 minutes. Turn over lobster halves and claws and spread each with some of the cilantro–chile butter; continue cooking until cooked through, about 3 minutes more. Serve with lime wedges.

## Lobster 101

With its sweet, succulent meat, the American lobster, *Humanus americanus*, is the most luxurious delicacy pulled from the cold waters of the North and Mid-Atlantic. It's also one of the easiest to cook if you follow a few simple guidelines. Figure on 1¼ to 2 lbs. of lobster per person, and buy only feisty live lobsters that feel heavy for their size from a fishmonger who keeps the specimens in aerated tanks. Some cooks elect to humanely kill lobsters before cooking by freezing them for 2 hours or by putting the lobster belly side down on a cutting board and slicing through the middle of the head with a sharp chef's knife or cleaver. If grilling or broiling, continue slicing all the way down the lobster through the tail, making sure to remove the gravel sac near the head and the vein that runs along the back.

# Poultry

These are the dishes that bring us together around the table: the oven-roasted chicken, with crackling herb-rubbed skin and juicy breast meat; the simmering pot of chicken stew rich with paprika and lashed with sour cream; Thai red curry, studded with duck. Across cultures, chicken and poultry are at the heart of the kitchen and are the centerpieces of some of our most soulful meals.

*Chef Sara Jenkins, with her son at her side, serves roasted chicken in her New York City home.*

# Lemony Roast Chicken

*Pollo Arrosto*

It sounds simple, and it is: nothing more than chicken, olive oil, rosemary, lemon, and garlic. But when chef Evan Kleiman began serving this rustic Italian-style roast chicken at Los Angeles's Angeli Caffe back in 1984, it turned out to be everything her customers were craving—honest food prepared with minimal fuss. Serve with rice or buttered noodles.

| | |
|---|---|
| 1 | 3½-lb. chicken, cut into 8 pieces |
| ½ | cup extra-virgin olive oil |
| ½ | cup fresh rosemary leaves |
| ¼ | cup fresh lemon juice |
| 10 | cloves garlic, thinly sliced |
| 1 | lemon, peel removed, pith and pulp chopped Kosher salt and freshly ground black pepper, to taste |

*Serves 4*

**1.** Toss the chicken pieces with the olive oil, rosemary, lemon juice, garlic, lemon, and salt and pepper to taste in a bowl. Marinate for about 1 hour.

**2.** Heat the oven to 475°F. Arrange the chicken in a 9 x 13-inch baking dish and add the remaining marinade. Roast, turning once, until cooked through, 30–40 minutes.

**3.** Divide chicken between 4 plates and serve.

## Family Style

Want to get to know your community? Open a neighborhood restaurant, and be lucky enough to have it stick around for a couple of decades. My little place in Los Angeles, Angeli Caffe, has been in business since 1984 on the wacky end of Hollywood's Melrose Avenue. The space was a former screen door shop that my partners and I turned into a restaurant with very little money and lots of good will. At the beginning, we were hip, so hip, feeding a generation of partying boomers who were eating out every night. But over the years, I watched our customers go from dancing fools to sleep-deprived new parents to mature stewards of a younger generation of tattooed hipsters. When I was growing up in L.A. in the 1960s, there was nowhere to get food like this; you couldn't even buy fresh basil at the supermarket. It wasn't until I went to Italy that I discovered the simple goodness of dishes like lemony roast chicken, dishes that most of us take for granted today. Opening Angeli was my way of bringing that kind of beautiful comfort food home, and connecting with the people I prepare it for. *—Evan Kleiman*

# Red-Chile Chicken Enchiladas

In southern New Mexico and neighboring El Paso, Texas, brick-red *chile colorado* salsa is the sauce of choice for enchiladas. We learned to make these from Malú Gonzales, a home cook in Las Cruces, New Mexico, who garnishes her enchiladas with a drizzle of cool *crema* and crumbled *cotija* cheese, a refreshing contrast to the gentle sting of the red chiles in the sauce.

Kosher salt, to taste

2 bone-in, skinless chicken legs

20 dried New Mexico chiles, stemmed and seeded

3 tbsp. canola oil, plus more for frying

10 cloves garlic, smashed

¼ cup fresh lime juice

1 tbsp. ground cumin

2 tsp. sugar

12 6-inch corn tortillas

2 cups shredded mozzarella

2 cups shredded sharp cheddar cheese

¾ cup minced red onion

¼ cup finely crumbled cotija cheese

2 tbsp. minced fresh cilantro for garnish

3 tbsp. crema or sour cream

*Serves 4–6*

**1.** Bring 6 cups of lightly salted water to a boil in a 4-qt. saucepan over medium-high heat. Add the chicken legs and reduce the heat to medium-low; simmer until the chicken is cooked through, about 35 minutes. Set a fine sieve over a bowl. Strain the chicken, reserving the cooking liquid. Let the chicken cool, then shred the meat, discarding the bones; set aside.

**2.** Meanwhile, soak the chiles in the reserved cooking liquid until softened, 20 minutes. Transfer the chiles and 2 cups of soaking liquid to a blender; set aside.

**3.** Heat the oven to 450°F. Heat 3 tbsp. oil in a 12-inch skillet over medium heat. Add the garlic cloves and cook, stirring often, until golden brown, about 2 minutes. Using a slotted spoon, transfer the garlic, reserving the oil in the skillet, to the blender with the chiles. Purée the chile–garlic mixture and then add the lime juice, cumin, and sugar and season with salt. Set a fine sieve over a bowl; strain the sauce, discarding the solids. Transfer the chile sauce to the reserved skillet and keep warm over medium-low heat.

**4.** Meanwhile, pour oil into a 10-inch skillet over medium-high heat to a depth of ½ inch. When the oil is hot, using tongs and working with 1 tortilla at a time, dip a tortilla in oil and cook until slightly crisp, about 15 seconds. Transfer the tortilla to a rack set over a rimmed baking sheet to drain. Dip the tortilla in the warm chile sauce to coat, and transfer to a plate. Sprinkle some of the shredded chicken, mozzarella, cheddar, and onions along the center of the tortilla and roll the tortilla to make an enchilada. Repeat with the remaining tortillas and chicken, reserving some of the cheese and onions.

**5.** Arrange the rolled enchiladas seam side down in a large casserole dish or on a rimmed baking sheet, pour over the remaining sauce, and sprinkle with the remaining mozzarella and cheddar. Bake until the cheese is melted, about 5 minutes. Garnish the enchiladas with the remaining onions, cotija cheese, and cilantro, drizzle with crema, and serve.

*Three generations of the Enriquez family—esteemed for their cooking—prepare dinner at their home in El Paso, Texas.*

## Special Sauce

The winning combination of succulent chicken and creamy, spice-laden tomato gravy known as chicken tikka masala has, over the years, become a comfort-food staple on Indian restaurant menus and in home kitchens around the world. Its beginnings are murky, though it likely originated in Great Britain in the 1970s, when an

Indian restaurant cook attempted to replicate a famous Delhi restaurant's signature dish, *murgh makhani* (butter chicken): tandoor-baked chicken in a sauce made with butter and tomatoes. Though some condemn the British riff on the dish, known as chicken tikka masala, as inauthentic (many recipes call for canned tomato soup, after all), I would argue that it belongs to a long and illustrious line of South Asian dishes that have been reinterpreted throughout the colonial and postcolonial eras, giving rise to a distinct, Anglo-Indian style of cookery. The dish's main component, chicken tikka, or boneless chicken pieces marinated in a mixture of yogurt and spices and then cooked in a clay tandoor oven, is itself a classic Punjabi dish. The tandoor imparts a smoky flavor to the chicken, which acquires a vivid orange or scarlet hue from turmeric, cayenne, or, often, food coloring in the marinade. Today, many chefs opt for fresh tomatoes instead of tomato soup; some also enrich the sauce with ground almonds and substitute more-fragrant coconut milk for cream. Home cooks, too, have furthered the evolution by grilling or broiling the chicken to reproduce the tandoor-baked flavor. While the exact lineage of chicken tikka masala remains a subject of debate, I regard it with affection as an example of the dynamic nature of Indian food. *—Lizzie Collingham*

# Chicken Tikka Masala

Thick tomato gravy makes a rich, creamy complement to juicy chicken with a hint of smoky flavor from the broiler; keeping the meat separate from the sauce until just before serving preserves its firm, succulent texture.

| | |
|---|---|
| 1 | tbsp. ground turmeric |
| 4 | tsp. garam masala |
| 1 | tsp. red food coloring (optional) |
| 6 | cloves garlic, crushed |
| 1 | 2½-inch piece ginger, peeled and chopped, plus julienned strips for garnish |
| 1 | jalapeño, stemmed and chopped |
| 1 | 28-oz. can whole peeled tomatoes, undrained |
| 2 | lbs. boneless, skinless chicken breasts, cut into 1½-inch cubes |
| ¼ | cup plain Greek yogurt Kosher salt, to taste |
| 6 | tbsp. unsalted butter |
| 1 | tsp. coriander seeds |
| ½ | tsp. cumin seeds |
| 1 | tbsp. paprika |
| 2 | small yellow onions, minced |
| 1 | cup heavy cream Fresh cilantro leaves, for garnish |
| 6 | cups cooked basmati rice, for serving |

*Serves 6*

**1.** In a blender, purée the turmeric, 2 tsp. garam masala, food coloring, garlic, ginger, jalapeños, and ½ cup water. Transfer the paste to a bowl. In the same blender, purée the tomatoes and strain through a sieve into a separate bowl; set aside.

**2.** In a bowl, mix 2 tbsp. of the reserved paste, along with the chicken cubes, yogurt, and salt; marinate for about 30 minutes. Place an oven rack 4 inches from the heating element; heat to broil. Transfer the chicken to a foil-lined baking sheet. Broil until cooked through, about 5 minutes; set aside.

**3.** Heat the butter in 6-qt. sauce-pan over medium-high heat. Add the coriander and cumin and toast for 4–6 minutes. Add the paprika and onions and cook until the onions are soft, 6–8 minutes. Add the remaining paste and brown for about 5 minutes. Add the tomatoes and cook for about 2 minutes. Stir in the cream and 1 cup water. Bring to a boil, then reduce the heat to medium-low and simmer until thickened, 6–8 minutes. Stir in the remaining garam masala and the broiled chicken; season with salt. Garnish with the julienned ginger and cilantro and serve over rice.

# Chicken Paprikash with Dumplings

*Paprikás Csirke*

When SAVEUR reader Isabelle Zgonc of Slippery Rock, Pennsylvania, sent us her family recipe for paprikash, Hungary's famous paprika-spiced braised chicken dish, she also shared some of the happy childhood memories it evokes for her. "It was good, hearty food that pleased all our senses," she recalled. Soft dumplings, sautéed with butter and parsley just before serving, are perfect for soaking up the paprikash's thick red sauce.

1    tsp. kosher salt, plus more to taste

2½   cups plus 2 tbsp. flour

1    egg, lightly beaten

1    3- to 4-lb. chicken, cut into 6–8 pieces, skin removed

    Freshly ground black pepper, to taste

¼    cup canola oil

2    tbsp. sweet paprika

1    Italian frying pepper, chopped

2    medium tomatoes, peeled, cored, seeded, and chopped

1    large yellow onion, minced

1½   cups chicken stock

¾    cup sour cream

3    tbsp. unsalted butter

2    tbsp. minced flat-leaf parsley

*Serves 4*

**1.** First, make the dumplings. Bring an 8-qt. stockpot of salted water to a boil. In a bowl, whisk together 2 cups of the flour and 1 tsp. of salt and form a well in the center. Add the egg and ½ cup water to the well and stir to form a dough. Knead dough in the bowl until smooth, about 1 minute. Using a teaspoon, scoop walnut-size portions of the dough into the pot of boiling water. Boil the dumplings until tender, 6–8 minutes. Drain the dumplings and rinse in cold water; cover with a tea towel and set aside.

**2.** Meanwhile, season the chicken with salt and pepper. Put ½ cup flour on a plate, dredge the chicken in the flour, and shake off the excess. Heat the oil in a 6-qt. Dutch oven over medium-high heat. Cook the chicken, turning once, until brown, 8–10 minutes. Remove the chicken and set aside.

**3.** Add the paprika and half the frying peppers, along with the tomatoes and onions, to the Dutch oven and cook, stirring, until the onions are soft, about 5 minutes. Add the reserved chicken and the stock and bring to a boil. Reduce the heat to medium-low and simmer, covered, turning the chicken once, until fully cooked, 12–15 minutes. In a small bowl, whisk together the remaining 2 tbsp. flour and the sour cream. Whisk in ¾ cup of the sauce from the pot. Stir the sour cream mixture back into the sauce in the pot. Remove from the heat.

**4.** Melt the butter in a 12-inch skillet over medium-high heat, add the reserved dumplings and the parsley, and cook, tossing occasionally, until hot, about 2 minutes. Serve the chicken garnished with the remaining frying peppers and dumplings on the side.

## Fit to Be Tied

Lemongrass is a tough-fibered aromatic herb that's used as a flavoring in countless dishes in Southeast Asia, including ones like Indonesian chicken curry. A stalk or two of the pale green herb infuses soups, braises, and curries with a citrusy taste. Lemongrass can be pulverized to make an ingredient in spice pastes or finely sliced for stir-fries, but it's often used in its whole form, in much the same way a bouquet garni is: dropped into the pot as a dish cooks and then removed at the end. First, trim the tip and the root end and peel away the stalk's fibrous outer layers. Next, use a meat mallet (or, in a pinch, the back of a kitchen knife) to smash and bruise the stalk until it's pliable. Finally, tie the stalk into a knot and put it into the pot.

# Indonesian Chicken Curry

*Opor Ayam*

In this dish, based on a recipe in SAVEUR editor-in-chief James Oseland's cookbook *Cradle of Flavor*, cinnamon and lemongrass lend vibrancy to the silky sauce.

| | |
|---|---|
| 1 | tbsp. coriander seeds |
| ½ | tsp. crushed red chile flakes |
| 2 | cloves garlic, chopped |
| 1 | medium yellow onion, chopped |
| 1 | 4-inch piece ginger, peeled and thinly sliced |
| 3 | tbsp. peanut oil |
| 5 | fresh or frozen Kaffir lime leaves |
| 4–6 | 4-inch sticks cinnamon |
| 1 | stalk lemongrass, smashed and tied into a knot (shown at left) |
| 3 | lbs. mixed chicken thighs and legs |
| 2 | cups coconut milk |
| ¾ | tsp. kosher salt |
| 4 | cups cooked jasmine rice, for serving |

*Serves 4–6*

**1.** Finely grind coriander and chile flakes in a spice grinder. Put spice mixture into a small food processor with garlic, onions, and ginger; purée to a paste. Add 1–2 tbsp. water, if necessary.

**2.** Heat oil in a 5-qt. Dutch oven over medium-low heat. Add paste; cook, stirring frequently, until fragrant, 5–7 minutes. Add lime leaves, cinnamon, and lemongrass. Cook, stirring occasionally, until cinnamon is fragrant, about 2 minutes. Increase heat to medium, add chicken, and cook, turning once, until golden brown, 8–10 minutes. Stir in 1 cup coconut milk, 1¼ cups water, and salt. Simmer, stirring occasionally, until chicken is tender, 40–50 minutes.

**3.** Add remaining coconut milk to the curry; cook for 2 minutes. Let cool for 20 minutes before serving with the rice.

# Sweet-and-Spicy Korean Fried Chicken

*Yangnyeom Dak*

The South Korea–based, internationally popular Kyochon restaurant chain guards its recipe for fried chicken closely, but we think we've managed to crack the code. Our version has the same spicy-tangy flavor and incomparable crunch.

|     |                                         |
|-----|-----------------------------------------|
|     | Canola oil, for frying                  |
| 5   | cloves garlic                           |
| 1   | ½-inch piece peeled ginger              |
| 3   | tbsp. soy sauce                         |
| 3   | tbsp. gojujang (Korean chile paste)     |
| 1½  | tbsp. rice vinegar                      |
| 1   | tbsp. Asian sesame oil                  |
| 1   | tbsp. honey                             |
| ⅔   | cup flour                               |
| 1   | tbsp. cornstarch                        |
| 16  | chicken wings or drumettes (about 1¾ lbs.) |

*Serves 2–4*

**1.** Pour oil into a 6-qt. pot to a depth of 2 inches and heat over medium-high heat until a deep-fry thermometer reads 350°F.

**2.** Mince the garlic and ginger in a food processor. Add the soy sauce, gojujang, vinegar, sesame oil, and honey and purée. Transfer the sauce to a bowl and set aside.

**3.** Whisk together the flour, cornstarch, and ⅔ cup water in another bowl. Add the chicken and toss to coat. Working in 3 batches, fry the chicken until golden, 6–8 minutes. Drain on paper towels.

**4.** Return the oil to 350°F. Fry the chicken until crisp, 6–8 minutes more. Drain again. Toss the chicken in the sauce and serve.

## The Other KFC

Twice-fried sweet-spicy chicken has long been a favorite in Korean homes and restaurants. Nineteen years ago in Gumi, South Korea, a restaurant owner named Kwon Won Kang added his own savory garlic-soy dressing to double-fried wings and drumsticks, and

the specialty known as *yangnyeom dak* (Korean fried chicken) took off as a fast-food phenomenon. Today, the business Kwon founded, called Kyochon, has more than 1,000 outlets worldwide, and Korean fried chicken has a global following. The restaurant's popularity is no surprise. Its wings and drumsticks are unfailingly juicy inside, crunchy outside, and glazed with one of two delicious sauces: hot-sweet or garlic–soy. A totally addictive food, it's lighter, less salty, and less greasy than American-style fried chicken. The key is in the precision frying. When an order comes in, a cook takes a batch of unseasoned wings and drumsticks—pared from small, fresh chickens and chilled overnight to decrease their moisture before frying—and dunks them in a thin batter of wheat flour, water, and cornstarch. Then he gives the wings and drumsticks a 9-minute sizzle in a deep-fryer containing 350°F canola oil, which cooks the meat and forms a light crust. Next, he tosses the chicken in a wire strainer to shake off loose bits of fried batter before plunging it into a second fryer, which contains oil left over from the previous day; the darker oil gives the skin a deeper flavor and hue. Three minutes later, the chicken emerges with a delicate texture and crackly crust that is ready to be sauced
—*Cathy Danh*

# Northern Fried Chicken

The fried chicken at Blue Ribbon (pictured at right), a restaurant in New York City, has a thick, crunchy crust made with matzo meal; the chefs there serve it with honey for dipping, collard greens quick-sautéed in brown butter, and mashed potatoes with gravy.

Canola oil, for frying
½ tsp. hot paprika
⅛ tsp. each cayenne pepper, dried basil, dried parsley, garlic powder, and onion powder
4 egg whites, beaten
½ cup flour
½ cup matzo meal
¼ tsp. baking powder
1 3-lb. chicken, cut into 8 pieces
Kosher salt and freshly ground black pepper, to taste
Honey, for dipping (optional)

*Serves 4*

**1.** Pour oil into a 5-qt. Dutch oven to a depth of 2 inches. Heat over medium-high heat until a deep-fry thermometer reads 375°F.

**2.** Combine paprika, cayenne, basil, parsley, and garlic and onion powders in a bowl; set aside. Put egg whites into a bowl. Combine flour, matzo, and baking powder in another bowl.

**3.** Working with one piece at a time, dip chicken in egg whites and press into matzo mixture to coat. Shake off excess; transfer chicken to a rack set inside a baking sheet. Working in 2 batches, fry chicken until crispy and cooked through, 10–12 minutes. Transfer chicken to paper towels and season with salt, pepper, and the reserved paprika mixture. Serve with honey, if you like.

# Roasted Herbed Chicken and Vegetables

The first step to making this traditional Sunday supper is to infuse melted butter with *herbes de Provence*, a mix of lavender, thyme, tarragon, sage, marjoram, and savory. After frequent basting with that herb butter during roasting, the chicken turns golden brown and intensely fragrant.

| | |
|---|---|
| 4 | tbsp. unsalted butter |
| 1½ | tbsp. dried herbes de Provence |
| 1 | tbsp. honey |
| 2 | cups white wine |
| ½ | cup extra-virgin olive oil |
| 1 | tbsp. fennel seeds |
| 12 | cloves garlic, unpeeled (8 whole, 4 crushed) |
| 3 | medium turnips, cut into 2-inch pieces |
| 1 | small butternut squash (about 1½ lbs.), peeled, seeded, and cut into thick half-moons |
| | Kosher salt and coarsely ground pepper, to taste |
| 1 | 4-lb. chicken |
| 1 | lemon |
| 1 | bunch thyme |
| 1 | large yellow onion, cut into thick wedges |
| ¾ | lb. Brussels sprouts, trimmed and halved |
| ¾ | lb. cremini mushrooms, left whole |
| 12 | large sage leaves |

*Serves 4*

**1.** Heat the oven to 375°F. Melt the butter and herbes de Provence in a pot over medium heat. Remove from heat; whisk in honey. Cover; let herb butter steep for 20 minutes. In a bowl, combine wine, half the oil, fennel, whole garlic, turnips, squash, and salt and pepper; set turnip mixture aside.

**2.** Season chicken with salt and pepper. Peel rind from lemon in strips. Halve lemon; set aside. Put rind into cavity with remaining garlic and thyme. Tie legs with twine; tuck wings under body; set chicken on a small roasting rack in a roasting pan. Arrange turnip mixture around chicken; scatter with onions. Brush chicken with some herb butter. Roast, basting chicken with herb butter and vegetables with pan juices, until turnips are just tender, about 1 hour.

**3.** Toss Brussels sprouts, mushrooms, and sage together in a bowl with remaining oil and salt and pepper; transfer to pan. Continue roasting until a thermometer inserted in chicken's thigh reads 165°F, 25–30 minutes. Transfer chicken to a platter; cover loosely with foil. Return vegetables to oven; roast until very tender, about 20 minutes more. Carve chicken (following steps shown at right), squeeze reserved lemon over top, and serve with vegetables.

## Carving a Chicken

A perfectly roasted chicken all but demands a deftly wielded knife and a sense of ceremony. The four steps below are easy to master and produce neat, elegant portions.

Ⓐ Set chicken on its side with the breast away from you. Place a fork against the thigh to steady chicken and, using a carving knife, cut between the body and the leg to begin to separate the two.

Ⓑ Pierce the breast with the fork to steady the chicken, and complete the separation of leg from body by working the knife through the connecting joint. Set the leg aside on the carving platter.

Ⓒ Hold the breast down with the fork. Using the knife, make an incision alongside the wishbone. Make a deep cut along the breastbone to remove breast meat. Halve and set aside on carving platter.

Ⓓ Separate the drumstick from the thigh by cutting through the connecting joint while holding the leg steady with the fork. Turn the chicken over and repeat preceding steps on the other side.

# Thai Red Curry with Roasted Duck

*Gaeng Phed*

The crisp-skinned roasted duck available in Chinatowns across America makes a great shortcut ingredient for many delicious, homey dishes, including this spicy-sweet Thai curry. Ask the counterperson at your local Chinese market to cut the roasted duck into bite-size pieces, which you can then simply toss into the simmering curry sauce.

| | |
|---|---|
| 2½ | cups canned unsweetened coconut milk |
| ¼ | cup Thai red curry paste, such as Mae Ploy brand |
| ½ | Chinese roasted duck, cut into 2-inch pieces |
| 10 | fresh or frozen Kaffir lime leaves |
| 1 | cup fresh pineapple, peeled, cored, and cut into 1-inch chunks |
| 1½ | tbsp. fish sauce |
| 1 | tbsp. Thai palm sugar |
| 6 | Thai chiles, stemmed |
| 20 | cherry tomatoes, left whole Leaves from 10 stems basil, preferably Thai basil |
| 4 | cups cooked jasmine rice, for serving |

*Serves 4*

**1.** Heat 1 cup of the coconut milk in a large pot over medium heat until it just begins to boil. Reduce the heat to medium-low and simmer, stirring often, until the liquid is slightly reduced, about 5 minutes. Whisk in the curry paste and continue to simmer the mixture, stirring occasionally, until the liquid is very aromatic, about 5 minutes more.

**2.** Add the cut-up duck to the curry mixture and increase the heat to medium. Cook, stirring occasionally, until the duck is heated through, about 7 minutes. Add the remaining coconut milk, lime leaves, and ¾ cup water. Increase the heat to medium-high, bring to a boil, then reduce the heat to medium-low. Simmer, stirring, until the flavors meld, about 2 minutes. Add the pineapple, fish sauce, palm sugar, and chiles and continue to simmer on medium-low heat, stirring occasionally, until the pineapple is fork-tender, about 5 minutes more.

**3.** Skim off and discard some of the oil from the top of the curry, if you like. Stir in the tomatoes and basil and simmer the curry for about 1 minute more; the tomatoes and basil should retain their shape and bright color. Serve the curry over steamed jasmine rice.

# Meats

Whether it's a juicy burger straight off the grill or some beautiful lamb chops we brought home from the butcher shop, our love of meat is all-consuming. This is food we treat ourselves with: a plate of meatballs braised in a rich tomato sauce; a flank steak, left to tenderize overnight in a spicy marinade, then grilled until it's charred at the edges and reddish-pink in the middle; a chicken fried steak, with its crispy coating and creamy gravy. At once nuanced and straightforward, these dishes sate us in an almost primal way.

*Owner Peter Servedio assists customers at Peter's Meat Market, a butcher shop on Arthur Avenue in the Bronx, New York.*

# Lamb Chops with Salsa Verde

Bracing mint cuts through lamb's richness. Cooks in Spain and Italy often combine mint with anchovies, red chile flakes, garlic, capers, and other herbs in a vibrant *salsa verde* like this one, a bold match for seared lamb chops.

| | |
|---|---|
| 4 | 1-inch-thick lamb loin chops (about 1 lb.) or frenched lamb rib chops |
| 2 | tbsp. plus ¾ cup extra-virgin olive oil |
| | Kosher salt and freshly ground black pepper, to taste |
| 2 | cups loosely packed fresh mint leaves, minced |
| ½ | cup minced flat-leaf parsley leaves |
| 2 | tbsp. minced fresh tarragon leaves |
| 1 | tbsp. salt-packed capers, soaked, rinsed, and minced |
| ¼ | tsp. crushed red chile flakes |
| 6 | oil-packed anchovy filets, drained and minced |
| 1 | clove garlic, minced |

*Serves 2*

**1.** Put the lamb chops into a small baking dish, rub with 2 tbsp. oil, and season with salt and pepper. Set aside to rest for 30 minutes.

**2.** Meanwhile, make the salsa verde: Combine the mint, parsley, tarragon, capers, chile flakes, anchovies, and garlic in a medium bowl. Slowly drizzle in the remaining oil while stirring with a fork; set aside.

**3.** Build a medium-hot fire in a charcoal grill or set a gas grill to medium-high heat. (Alternatively, heat a cast-iron grill pan over medium-high heat.) Add the lamb chops and cook, turning once, until well browned and crusty and cooked to the desired doneness, 6–8 minutes for medium rare if using loin chops; about 4 minutes if using rib chops. Transfer the lamb chops to a platter. Stir the sauce and drizzle over the chops, reserving some of the sauce to serve on the side.

## Lamb Varieties

The flavor and the texture of lamb can differ considerably from place to place, reflecting everything from what the animals eat to the physical characteristics of particular breeds. Because sheep farming remains a small industry in the United States when compared with those of beef and pork, your local supermarket is as likely to carry cuts of lamb raised in Australia or New Zealand—the world's top lamb-exporting countries—as it is fresh domestic meat. Most New Zealand lamb is almost entirely pasture fed, usually in fields rich with ryegrass and clover, which accounts for the meat's characteristic leanness. Because New Zealand lambs come to market very young, typically at only six or seven months of age, they have smaller frames that yield petite, tender rib chops. Australian lamb, though it's slaughtered when a bit older, has a milder taste and richer marbling—the results of both breeding and the fact that the animals are sometimes fed grain during the last weeks of their lives. Free-range, grass-fed Icelandic lamb is exceptionally fine-grained and mild tasting; it is prized by chefs and increasingly sold in the United States at stores like Whole Foods Market. Most varieties of American lamb are crossbred from wool breeds like Columbia and meat breeds such as Suffolk and are raised in the high rangelands of the Western states. Colorado lamb, one of the predominant domestic varieties, is pasture fed and given a diet of corn before slaughter to make it yield princely cuts of richly marbled meat.

# Seven-Hour Leg of Lamb

*Gigot de Sept Heures*

Roasting a leg of lamb for a full seven hours in wine with garlic and herbs leaves the meat ultratender; white beans stewed with thyme, cloves, and onion and finished with crème fraîche are a luxurious accompaniment. This recipe was given to us by Parisian home cook Camille Labro (pictured at center of top left photograph on facing page), who learned it from her Provençale mother.

**FOR THE LAMB:**

- 1    4-lb. shank end leg of lamb or 4-lb. piece of shoulder, trimmed
- 3    tbsp. extra-virgin olive oil Kosher salt and freshly ground black pepper, to taste
- 1    750-ml bottle dry white wine
- 20   cloves garlic, unpeeled
- 10   sprigs each fresh thyme, rosemary, and savory
- 5    fresh or dried bay leaves

**FOR THE BEANS:**

- 2    cups dried white beans, preferably cannellini or white coco, soaked overnight
- 5    cloves garlic, smashed
- 3    sprigs fresh thyme and parsley and a bay leaf tied together with kitchen twine
- 10   whole cloves
- 1    large onion, halved Kosher salt and freshly ground black pepper, to taste
- 2    tbsp. extra-virgin olive oil
- 2    tbsp. crème fraîche

*Serves 6–8*

**1.** Cook the lamb: Heat the oven to 300°F. Rub lamb with oil and season generously with salt and pepper. Heat a 6-qt. Dutch oven over medium-high heat. Add lamb and cook, turning occasionally, until browned on all sides, about 12 minutes. Transfer lamb to a plate. Add wine and 2 cups water to the Dutch oven; scrape up browned bits from bottom of pot. Nestle garlic and herbs into a large oval casserole and place lamb on top of herbs. Carefully pour in pan juices and wine from Dutch oven and cover lamb with foil. Transfer to oven and roast, basting frequently, for 3½ hours.

Uncover, flip lamb, and continue to cook, basting frequently, until lamb is very tender, 3–3½ more hours. Transfer to a rack and let cool for 20 minutes.

**2.** Meanwhile, prepare the beans: About 1½ hours before the lamb is done, drain beans and transfer to a 4-qt. saucepan along with 4 cloves garlic, the herb bundle, and 6 cups water. Pierce the onion with the cloves and add to the pot. Bring to a boil, reduce heat to low, cover, and simmer until beans are tender, about 1 hour. Remove pot from heat and season with salt and pepper. Discard herbs and strain beans, reserving cooking liquid. Transfer 2 cups beans, ¼ cup cooking liquid, oil, crème fraîche, and remaining garlic clove to a blender and purée. Stir puréed bean mixture and about 1 cup of the cooking liquid back into pot and cover to keep warm until lamb is cooked. Serve the lamb sliced or torn into chunks, alongside the beans.

# Marinated Flank Steak

Flank steak, also known as London broil, isn't the most tender cut of beef, but it is one of the most flavorful. The key to getting a tender flank steak is to let the meat marinate for a good, long time—in this case, in a mixture of red wine, Worcestershire sauce, garlic, various spices, and fresh rosemary—and then carve it across the grain into thin slices before serving.

| | |
|---|---|
| 1 | tbsp. black peppercorns |
| 1 | tbsp. coriander seeds |
| 1 | tbsp. fennel seeds |
| 2 | dried chiles de árbol, broken |
| 2 | bay leaves |
| ½ | cup red wine |
| 2 | tbsp. red wine vinegar |
| 2 | tbsp. Worcestershire |
| 4 | cloves garlic, crushed |
| 2 | sprigs fresh rosemary |
| ½ | cup extra-virgin olive oil |
| 1 | 2-lb. flank steak |
| | Kosher salt, to taste |

*Serves 4*

**1.** Toast the peppercorns, coriander, fennel, chiles de árbol, and bay leaves in a small skillet over high heat, stirring occasionally, until fragrant, 2–3 minutes. Transfer the aromatics to a hard surface, lightly crush them with the bottom of a heavy skillet, then transfer them to a 9 x 13-inch baking dish.

**2.** Add the wine, vinegar, Worcestershire, garlic, rosemary, and olive oil to the baking dish and whisk to combine. Prick the steak all over with a fork, place it in the marinade and spoon some marinade over the top. Cover and refrigerate, turning occasionally, for at least 12 hours and up to 24 hours.

**3.** An hour before grilling, transfer the steak to a plate, season with salt, and set aside at room temperature. Transfer the marinade to a small pot and bring just to a boil; set aside.

**4.** Build a medium-hot fire in a charcoal grill or set a gas grill to medium-high heat. Grill the steak, turning once and, using a brush, basting with the reserved marinade occasionally, until browned and medium rare, 7–8 minutes per side. Transfer the steak to a cutting board, tent with foil, and let rest for about 10 minutes. Carve the steak into thin slices across the grain and serve with any accumulated juices.

## Is It Done Yet?

When it comes to cooking a steak, most restaurant cooks have the seemingly magical ability to take the meat off the heat at exactly the right moment. For most of us at home, however, learning to cook a steak to perfection is a process of trial and error. But take heart: you don't need X-ray vision to divine the color of the inside of a thick steak; just some basic know-how. The same rules apply to all cuts, whether it's a flavorful flank (like the one pictured at left) or a pricey porterhouse: steaks become firmer and lose their red color as they cook, proceeding from "blue" (nearly raw) to rare (deep red) to medium rare (deep pink) to medium (light pink) to medium well (gray with a hint of pink) to well-done (gray throughout). Many cooks agree that medium rare is usually the level that brings out a steak's best qualities, in both flavor and texture. The most important thing to remember is that steaks cook fast (especially those from lean, grass-fed cattle). A meat thermometer usually isn't a good option for gauging doneness, since it's hard to get a reliable reading using most standard models. Also, following many published guidelines for judging doneness by temperature—including those issued by the USDA—will pretty much ensure that your steak is over-cooked. Some cooks determine the doneness of a steak by checking firmness—an old rule says a rare steak should feel like the soft flesh between your thumb and forefinger. Others follow a ten-minutes-per-inch rule. But for our money— and when we're shelling out for good meat, that's not an inconsiderable factor—the single best solution is the tried-and-true "nick and peek" method. Make a small cut in the steak, take a look inside, and judge the color for yourself. Until you've confidently mastered your own method, though, err on the side of caution and remove the steak from the heat slightly before you think it has achieved its desired doneness; it will continue to cook as it rests. And keep in mind that with thicker steaks, lean cuts (like a filet mignon) cook faster than fattier ones (like a rib eye) and that the presence of a bone prolongs the cooking time.

*A cowboy rides herd at La Cense ranch, an 88,000 acre grass-fed cattle operation in Dillon, Montana.*

# Italian-Style Meatballs with Tomato Ragù

There are many ways to make meatballs. This is, hands down our favorite. The recipe calls not only for ground pork shoulder and beef chuck but also for prosciutto, ricotta, and bacon. The meatballs are browned in a skillet, braised in red wine and tomatoes until they're succulent and suffused with sauce, then showered with minced parsley and grated cheese. Serve with crusty bread or spaghetti.

| | |
|---|---|
| 10 | oz. ground beef chuck |
| 10 | oz. ground pork shoulder |
| 2 | oz. prosciutto, minced |
| 2 | oz. minced pork fat or pancetta |
| 1¼ | cups loosely packed flat-leaf parsley leaves, minced, plus more to garnish |
| 2 | tsp. dried oregano |
| 1½ | tsp. fennel seeds |
| 1 | tsp. crushed red chile flakes |
| ½ | tsp. ground cumin |
| ¼ | tsp. ground allspice |
| 7 | slices white bread, finely ground in a food processor Kosher salt and freshly ground black pepper, to taste |
| ⅔ | cup ricotta, drained in a strainer for 2 hours |
| 2 | tbsp. milk |
| 3 | eggs, lightly beaten |
| 6 | tbsp. extra-virgin olive oil, plus more for greasing |
| ¼ | cup dry red wine |
| 4 | cups canned tomato purée |
| 1 | cup beef or veal stock Finely grated Parmigiano-Reggiano, for garnish |

*Serves 6*

**1.** In a large bowl, combine the beef, pork, prosciutto, pork fat, parsley, oregano, fennel seeds, chile flakes, cumin, allspice, and bread crumbs and season with salt. Using your fingers, mix the ingredients gently until combined, then set aside. In a medium bowl, whisk together the ricotta, milk, and eggs until smooth, then add to the meat mixture and gently mix until incorporated. Refrigerate the mixture for about 1 hour.

**2.** Heat the oven to 300°F. Grease 2 large rimmed baking sheets with oil and set aside. Using a 2-oz. ice cream scoop, portion the mixture, roll into meatballs with your hands, and transfer to the greased baking sheets.

**3.** Heat 3 tbsp. oil in a 3-qt. high-sided skillet over medium-high heat. Add half the meatballs and cook, turning occasionally, until browned, about 10 minutes. Using a slotted spoon, transfer the meatballs to a plate. Repeat with the remaining oil and meatballs.

**4.** Add the reserved meatballs back to the skillet along with any juices from the plate. Add the wine, increase the heat to high, and cook for 2 minutes. Stir in tomatoes and beef stock, bring to a boil, and tightly cover the skillet. Transfer to the oven and bake until the meatballs are tender and have absorbed some of the sauce, about 1½ hours.

**5.** Divide the meatballs between 6 serving bowls, top each serving with some of the sauce, and garnish with Parmigiano-Reggiano and parsley.

# Filets Mignons with Mushroom Sauce

A concentrated mushroom sauce made with red wine and sherry brings intense flavor to filet mignon, a mild-tasting and especially tender cut.

| | |
|---|---|
| 6 | tbsp. unsalted butter, cut into small pieces |
| 3 | tbsp. extra-virgin olive oil |
| 4 | 8-oz. filets mignons |
| | Kosher salt and freshly ground black pepper, to taste |
| 2 | shallots, minced |
| 1 | lb. cremini mushrooms, sliced |
| 1 | cup red wine |
| 1 | cup chicken stock |
| 2 | tbsp. sherry |
| 2 | tsp. cornstarch, mixed with 1 tbsp. water |
| 1 | tbsp. chopped chives |
| 1 | tbsp. chopped parsley |

*Serves 4*

**1.** Heat the oven to 500°F. Heat 1 tbsp. butter and 1 tbsp. oil in a 12-inch skillet over high heat. Season filets with salt and pepper and add to skillet; cook, flipping once, until browned, 4–5 minutes. Transfer filets to a baking sheet, reserving skillet, and roast in oven until medium rare, 4–5 minutes. Transfer filets to a platter and cover with aluminum foil.

**2.** Return skillet to medium-high heat. Add 1 tbsp. butter, the remaining oil, and shallots and cook for 1 minute; add mushrooms and cook, stirring occasionally, until softened, about 5 minutes. Add red wine, reduce heat to medium, and cook, stirring occasionally, until syrupy, about 8–10 minutes. Add stock and cook until slightly reduced, 4–5 minutes. Whisk in sherry and cornstarch mixture and bring to a boil; cook, stirring often, until thickened, 2–3 minutes. Remove pan from heat. Whisk in remaining butter, chives, and parsley and season with salt and pepper. Serve filets with mushroom sauce.

## Making the Grade

The passion for prime steak is fueled by how little of it there is to go around. Less than 4 percent of all beef that passes through USDA gradings—which, unlike safety inspection, is voluntary and paid for by the meat processor—is labeled prime, and most of that ends up being sold in high-end butcher shops, or served by waiters at pricey steak houses (such as Karl Zartler, pictured on the facing page, at New York City's famed Peter Luger Steak House). Among the criteria for inclusion in this elite tier are fat marbling (the more the better) and the animal's age (younger animals have less collagen in their muscle and, thus, meat that's more tender).

There are eight government grades for beef: prime, choice, select, standard, commercial, utility, canner, and cutter. Steak aficionados seek out the top two, prime and choice (the latter of which represents more than half of all graded beef), which are streaked with plenty of intramuscular fat—a condition that makes them tender enough for dry-heat cooking methods like grilling, roasting, and broiling. Steaks that have been graded select—a variety primarily sold in supermarkets—are generally too lean to yield better than average results. The remaining grades designate meat that's sold wholesale for use in a range of products, from frozen foods to hot dogs.

In addition to the federal grading system, consumers have another option available to them: beef that has undergone certification. This program, overseen by the USDA, certifies that the beef bearing the designation is from a particular breed or variety. The most common breed certification is for beef from Angus steer and heifers, which have consistently demonstrated a predisposition for developing well-marbled meat.

Steak lovers on a budget should remember that they'll get tastier results using lesser cuts (top round or flank steak, for example) graded prime or choice than they will with higher-end cuts (like rib eye or porterhouse) graded select. Note that most beef from grass-fed or "organic" animals is sold ungraded, as its quality can't be judged by the same standards that apply to commercial beef.

# Pineapple–Chipotle-Glazed Ham

New York chef Zarela Martinez gave us the idea for this glaze made from Coca-Cola, chipotle chiles, and honey—which caramelizes during roasting to produce a burnished, smoky-sweet exterior. Many home cooks in Martinez's native Mexico use cola in this way, to bring sweetness and cinnamon notes to braised and roasted meats. If you're using fresh pineapple slices, make perfect rings by using a 3-inch round cookie cutter to trim the outer edges and a 1-inch round one for the center.

| | |
|---|---|
| 1 | 12–15-lb. whole semiboneless ham |
| 8 | fresh or canned pineapple slices |
| 64 | whole cloves |
| 2¾ | cups Coca-Cola |
| 2 | chipotle chiles in adobo, drained and minced |
| ⅓ | cup honey |

*Serves 14–20*

**1.** Put the ham into a 16-qt. stockpot and cover with water. Bring to a boil, reduce the heat to medium-low, and simmer for 1 hour.

**2.** Heat the oven to 350°F. Transfer the ham to a rack in a roasting pan. Using toothpicks, secure the pineapple slices to the ham and stud with the cloves. Pour 2 cups Coca-Cola over the ham and pour 1 cup water into the roasting pan. Cover the ham loosely with foil and bake for 1 hour.

**3.** Meanwhile, combine the remaining Coca-Cola, chipotles, and honey in a saucepan and bring to a boil over medium-high heat. Reduce the heat to medium and cook, stirring the glaze, until syrupy, 12–15 minutes. Uncover the ham and brush with some of the glaze. Increase the oven temperature to 500°F. Bake the ham, brushing occasionally with the glaze, until browned and glossy, 15–20 minutes. Let cool for about 20 minutes before carving.

Giovedì 10 Gennaio 2008

| | SUGO DI CARNE | SUGO DI CODA | PESTO ALLA GENOVESE | CACIO E PEPE / CACIO PEPE E RICOTTA |
|---|---|---|---|---|
| FETTUCCINE | | | | |
| AGNOLOTTI | | | | |
| BRODO DI CARNE | | | | |
| GNOCCHI | | | | |

LOMBATA AI FERRI
POLPETTE AL SUGO
POLPETTE CON PISELLI
STRACCETTI CON CARCIOFI
FEGATO ALLA PIASTRA
CODA ALLA VACCINARA
SALSICCE ALLA PIASTRA
CARCIOFI ALLA GIUDIA
CARCIOFI ALLA ROMANA
BROCCOLI ATTUFATI AL VINO
MELANZANE GRIGLIATE
PUNTARELLE IN SALSA D'ACCIUGHE
INSALATA MISTA
CACIO CON LE PERE
ARANCIO CON ACCONDITO
FAGIOLI ACCONDITI
TORTA DI RICOTTA E VISCIOLE O RICOTTA E
GOCCE DI CIOCCOLATO
CIAMBELLINE AL VINO CON VINSANTO
RICOTTA DI PECORA CON NUTELLA GIANDUIOTTI
BIANCANERA DI SORA MARGHERITA
SACHER
TORTA CON CREMA DI ...

# Sweet and Sour Pork Chops

*Maiale in Agrodolce*

These grilled pork chops with a glaze of honey and balsamic vinegar are typical of the sturdy, lusty food found in Roman neighborhood restaurants (such as the 51-year-old Sora Lella, pictured at left) and home kitchens alike. They pair well with stewed sweet peppers, roasted potatoes, or sautéed greens.

| | |
|---|---|
| 4 | 10-oz. bone-in pork chops, frenched |
| 3 | tbsp. extra-virgin olive oil |
| | Kosher salt and freshly ground black pepper, to taste |
| ⅓ | cup balsamic vinegar |
| 2 | tbsp. honey |
| 1 | tbsp. unsalted butter |
| 1 | sprig fresh rosemary, torn into 1-inch pieces |

*Serves 4*

**1.** Put pork chops on a plate and drizzle with oil. Season the chops generously with salt and pepper and let sit for 30 minutes.

**2.** Meanwhile, build a medium-hot fire in a charcoal grill or heat a gas grill to medium-high heat. Combine vinegar and honey in a 1 qt. saucepan and cook over medium heat until reduced to ¼ cup. Add butter and rosemary, stir until butter is melted, and set aside.

**3.** Put pork chops on grill and cook, occasionally turning and basting with balsamic mixture, until browned and just cooked through, 12–14 minutes. Transfer to a platter and let sit for 5 minutes before serving.

## Local Specialty

One reason to visit Sid's Diner (pictured below) in El Reno, Oklahoma, is the hospitality. A small town 35 miles west of Oklahoma City, El Reno is the kind of place where nice-guy burger joint operators like Marty Hall are local celebrities. The other reason to visit Sid's, of course, is to eat the onion burger, the best of a local breed that was invented in El Reno during the Great Depression. The burger's distinguishing feature—lots and lots of onions cooked right into the patty— began as a way of stretching ground beef. Marty, who started making the specialty as a grill cook 41 years ago, places a small ball of beef on a hot flattop griddle, showers the meat with a heap of thinly sliced Vidalia onions, and then presses the patty down until the onions and beef become one. When the burger is crunchy and browned on the bottom, it's flipped so that the same thing can happen to the other side. The last time I was at Sid's, I asked Marty whether his burgers had changed over the years. "Cooking burgers is like laying brick," he told me. "Your best comes with years of experience. It becomes like an art." —*George Motz*

# Sid's Fried Onion Burgers

Onions are a classic burger topping, but at Sid's Diner in El Reno, Oklahoma, they are an integral element of the patty itself. Squashing the ground beef and onions together into the hot skillet results in a well-seared exterior, crisp edges, and a delectable caramelized-onion flavor.

| | |
|---|---|
| 1 | lb. ground beef |
| 2 | medium Vidalia or yellow onions |
| 4 | tbsp. canola oil Kosher salt, to taste |
| 6 | slices American cheese (optional) |
| 6 | hamburger buns, toasted Dill pickle slices |

*Makes 6 burgers*

**1.** Divide the ground beef into 6 equal balls, making sure to handle the meat gently. Very thinly slice the onions on a mandoline, or slice them using a sharp knife; divide the onions into 6 equal portions.

**2.** Working in two batches, heat 2 tbsp. of the oil in a 12-inch cast-iron skillet over medium-high heat. Add 3 of the beef balls and, using the back of a spatula, press down on them until they are thin. Cook for 1 minute. Top each patty with a portion of the onions, then season with salt. Press the onions into the meat and cook for about 1 minute more.

**3.** Flip the onion-topped patties and flatten them with the spatula. Place a cheese slice, if using, on each patty and let the cheese melt while the onions and meat brown. Top the bottom half of each bun with the onions and cheese-topped patties, add the top bun, and serve with dill pickle slices, if you like.

## Building the Perfect Burger

It just might be the ultimate comfort food: a juicy hamburger customized to appeal to our particular tastes and cravings. There's almost no limit to what works well when crafting a delicious burger; countless toppings and types of buns provide a pleasing contrast in taste, texture, and temperature. Maybe you're in the mood for a classic cheeseburger with some crisp, cool lettuce and raw red onion. Or something more decadent: blue cheese, sweet caramelized onion, and smoky bacon. Here are some of our favorite burger building blocks.

**Multiseed bun** Burger's answer to the everything bagel.

**Roasted peppers** Gives burgers a smoky, sweet accent.

**English muffin** Sturdy and soaks up juices like a sponge.

**Bibb lettuce** A velvety alternative to crunchy iceberg.

**American cheese** Sunny yellow, quick-melting, presliced. Classic.

**Kaiser roll** Bulky, with a fluffy interior perfect for juicy burgers.

**Caramelized onions** Give burgers a rich, decadent note.

**Sesame seed bun** Soft and fragrant, the iconic burger platform.

**Pickled beets** An earthy alternative to sweet pickles.

**Olive tapenade** Lends burgers a briny, Mediterranean quality.

**Potato roll** This sweet pillowy roll makes the softest of buns.

**Brie** Takes on a silky texture and a rich aroma when melted.

**Onion roll** Studded with onion, brings flavor to simple burgers.

**Red onion** A crisp, spicy, and robust addition.

**Limburger** This strong washed-rind cheese adds pungency.

**Bacon** Cured pork of all types adds a smoky taste.

**Cornichons** Lends a slightly sour flavor and snap.

**Sautéed mushrooms** Bolsters a burger's savory qualities.

**Pineapple rings** Introduces a refreshing, tangy sweetness.

**Pretzel roll** Salty, chewy; great with strong-flavored toppings.

**Blue cheese** Bold tartness balanced by a creamy texture.

**Coleslaw** Cool and creamy, gives crunch to burgers.

**French roll** A white, dense interior with a crisp crust.

**Alfalfa sprouts** Their fresh, grassy taste pairs well with beef.

**Toasted bread** Dense-textured bread is classic for a patty melt.

**Emmentaler** A Swiss cheese with a luscious, even melt.

**Pepper Jack** Flecked with jalapeños, this lends a spicy edge.

**Ciabatta roll** Thick-crusted; supports the juiciest of burgers.

**Tomato** A bright, sweet presence between burger and bun.

**Peperoncini** These brined peppers bring mild heat.

# Patty Melt

This lunch counter favorite—ground beef, caramelized onions, and melted cheese between slices of rye bread—is easy to make at home. Beyond the sliced bread that replaces the standard hamburger bun, what sets the patty melt apart is the fact that the whole thing, bread and all, is buttered and fried in a skillet after the patties have been cooked, for a result that's half grilled cheese, half burger.

1½    lbs. ground beef
      Kosher salt and freshly
      ground black pepper,
      to taste
5    tbsp. canola oil
2    medium yellow onions,
      halved and thinly sliced
12   slices rye bread
12   thin slices cheddar, Swiss,
      or American cheese
8    tbsp. unsalted butter,
      softened
      Pickles, for serving
      (optional)

*Serves 6*

**1.** Season the beef with salt and pepper. Divide the meat into six ¼-inch-thick patties that are slightly wider and longer than the bread slices. Set aside.

**2.** Heat 2 tbsp. oil in a 12-inch cast-iron skillet over medium-high heat. Add the onions, season with salt and pepper, and cook, stirring occasionally, until softened and browned, 10–12 minutes. Transfer the onions to a bowl; wipe out the skillet. Working in 3 batches, heat 1 tbsp. oil in the same skillet over high heat. Add 2 burger patties and cook, flipping once, until well browned, about 4 minutes total. Repeat with remaining patties. Transfer the patties to a plate.

**3.** Top each of 6 bread slices with some of the onions, a cheese slice, and a burger patty. Top each burger with a cheese slice and a piece of bread. Using a butter knife, spread butter over the top and bottom of each sandwich.

**4.** Heat a 12-inch nonstick skillet over medium heat. Working in 3 batches, cook the sandwiches, flipping once, until golden brown and warmed throughout, about 6 minutes. Serve with pickles, if you like.

## Texas Classic

The best chicken fried steak in Paradise, Texas, looks like it's covered in corn flakes and comes with peppery cream gravy. I'm talking about the one served at a place called the Finish Line Café. What brought me to the Finish Line was not just a deep love for CFS (as the dish is often called) but also a strong hunch. Driving around the state researching CFS, I'd begun to suspect that you could get a great version in just about any small-town café west of Dallas and north of Waco—an area of Texas I'd come to dub the Chicken Fried Steak Belt. I decided to test this theory by picking a random town along my planned route. Paradise (population 519) sounded like as good a spot as any, and the Finish Line Café was the most popular place in town.

There are three categories of CFS in Texas—German, Cowboy, and Southern—and each has its proponents who believe it's the original. According to Jane and Michael Stern's book *Eat Your Way Across the U.S.A.*, "chicken fried steak was a Depression-era invention of Hill Country German-Texans." German-style CFS is made of pounded-thin beef cube steak, dredged in bread crumbs or cracker meal and fried like schnitzel. The cowboy version is often called pan-fried steak in West Texas, where it's the most popular style. It's said that chuckwagon cooks, who tenderized their steaks by beating them with anything handy, would simply dredge them in flour before frying them to a crisp. Southern-style CFS, has a thick, crunchy buttermilk batter crust that looks like the coating on a piece of fried chicken; this is the style most common in East Texas, and it was the style that I became smitten with at the Finish Line.

The dish, prepared from a family recipe, was cooked by Marie Brown, the matriarch of the three generations who run the café (her daughter, Rayanne Gentry, is pictured at right). Dredged in seasoned flour, then in a batter of eggs and buttermilk, then in the flour again, Marie's steak emerged from the kitchen with an awesome, ripply crust that shattered when I bit through to the tender steak. This was the ultimate CFS: I was in paradise, indeed.
—*Robb Walsh*

# Chicken Fried Steak

There's more than one way to cook a chicken fried steak, that Texan creation of cube steak pounded out thin and tender, dipped in a buttermilk batter, and fried until it forms a thick, crunchy crust. Our favorite one comes from the Finish Line Café in Paradise, Texas, where they serve it smothered in a thick cream gravy.

2 cups plus 3 tbsp. flour
2 tsp. paprika
  Freshly ground black pepper and kosher salt, to taste
1 cup buttermilk
1 tsp. Tabasco, plus more to taste
1 egg
4 4–6-oz. cube steaks, pounded to ¼-inch thickness
  Canola oil, for frying
3 tbsp. unsalted butter
2 cups milk

*Serves 4*

**1.** Heat the oven to 200°F. Put a baking sheet fitted with a rack inside. In a shallow dish, whisk together 2 cups flour, paprika, pepper, and salt. In another dish, whisk together buttermilk, 1 tsp. Tabasco, and egg. Season steaks with salt and pepper. Working with 1 steak at a time, dredge in flour mixture, then in egg mixture, and again in flour; shake off excess. Transfer to a plate.

**2.** Pour oil into a 12-inch cast-iron skillet to a depth of ½ inch; heat over medium-high heat until a deep-fry thermometer reads 320°F. Working in 2 batches, fry steaks, flipping once, until golden brown, 6–8 minutes. Place steaks on rack in oven to keep warm.

**3.** Melt butter in a 2-qt. saucepan over medium-high heat. Whisk in remaining flour; cook until golden, 1–2 minutes. Whisk in milk; cook, whisking, until thick. Season with Tabasco and salt and pepper. Serve steaks with gravy.

# Slow-Smoked Brisket

Brisket is the king of Texas barbecue, thanks in part to mid-19th-century German and Czech immigrants who sold deli-style smoked brisket in the meat markets they opened in the central part of the state, a few of which are still in operation. You don't have to be a pit master to make good barbecued brisket; perfectly delicious results can be achieved at home, in an ordinary kettle grill. Here's how to do it.

1½ tbsp. kosher salt
1½ tbsp. dark brown sugar
1 tbsp. sweet paprika
2 tsp. garlic powder
2 tsp. mustard powder
1½ tsp. freshly ground black pepper
½ tsp. dried thyme
½ tsp. ground coriander
½ tsp. ground cumin
1 5-lb. flat-cut beef brisket with ½-inch fat left attached
3 large chunks mesquite wood
¾ cup beer

*Serves 6–8*

**1.** In a small bowl, stir together salt, brown sugar, paprika, garlic powder, mustard, pepper, thyme, coriander, and cumin; rub spice blend into brisket with your fingers to cover evenly; wrap tightly in plastic wrap. Refrigerate overnight.

**2.** Build a medium-hot charcoal fire in a grill.

**3.** When coals are ready, push them to one side of grill and nestle the chunks of mesquite around them.

**4.** Cover grill, open all vents, and let grill heat until temperature registers 225°–250°F on an instant-read thermometer inserted in a top vent.

**5.** Arrange a foil pan half-filled with water on the bottom grate opposite the coals, put the top grill grate in place, and set brisket on top grill grate directly over foil pan.

**6.** Cover grill and cook brisket, replenishing coals as needed to maintain a 225°–250°F temperature, until meat registers 160°F on an instant-read thermometer, 4–5 hours.

**7.** Transfer brisket to a sheet of heavy-duty aluminum foil and pour beer on top.

**8.** Wrap brisket in foil to seal in juices and beer. Return brisket to grill over pan, and cook, replenishing coals as needed, until meat reaches 190°F, about 2 hours more; uncover grill and let brisket cool for 1 hour.

**9.** Unwrap and arrange brisket, fat side up, on a cutting board, and slice across the grain into ⅛-inch-thick slices. Collect the juices and pour over meat before serving.

# Roast Pork Loin

*Arista di Maiale*

Stuffing a butterflied pork loin with herbs and wrapping it with prosciutto, a classic Tuscan preparation, keeps the meat juicy and bolsters its flavor. After roasting, let the meat rest to allow the moisture concentrated in the center during cooking to infuse the entire loin, and then serve it with a pan sauce made with fresh lemon juice.

| | |
|---|---|
| 1 | lemon |
| 5 | tbsp. chopped fresh rosemary |
| 25 | fresh sage leaves, minced |
| 12 | cloves garlic, minced |
| 1 | 4-lb. boneless pork loin, trimmed |
| 12 | thin center-cut slices prosciutto di Parma (3 oz.) Kosher salt and freshly ground black pepper, to taste |
| 2 | tbsp. extra-virgin olive oil |
| 1 | large onion, cut into thick rings |

*Serves 8–10*

**1.** Heat oven to 375°F. Zest lemon, slice in half, and set aside. Pile zest, rosemary, sage, and garlic on a cutting board and chop them together with a knife until combined. Set the herb mixture aside.

**2.** Butterfly the pork loin: Place pork loin perpendicular to you on a work surface. Using a long knife, start cutting into the meat along its long edge, keeping knife roughly ½ inch above the work surface. Continue slicing inward so that the meat unrolls and splays open. Set pork to the side and arrange ten 16-inch-long pieces of kitchen twine perpendicular to you, each one spaced ½ inch from the next; lay one 36-inch-long piece of twine across the shorter lengths. Lay 6 slices of prosciutto side by side atop and parallel to the short lengths of twine. Season both sides of pork loin with salt and pepper and rub both sides with herb mixture.

**3.** Roll pork into a cylinder and place it on top of prosciutto slices. Lay 6 more prosciutto slices over pork, tucking edges of bottom slices under top ones. Transfer prosciutto-wrapped pork loin to sit on top of prepared lengths of twine. Bring ends of long piece of twine up over pork loin, pull twine taut, and tie ends together. Bring ends of each short piece of twine together, pull taut, and tie together. Trim excess twine and discard.

**4.** Heat oil in a 12-inch ovenproof skillet over medium-high heat. Add pork roast and cook, turning occasionally, until browned on all sides, about 12 minutes. Transfer pork to a plate. Nestle onion slices in skillet and pour in ½ cup water; put pork on top of onions. Roast, basting occasionally with pan juices, until an instant-read thermometer inserted into middle of roast registers 140°F, about 45–50 minutes.

**5.** Transfer pork to a cutting board; let rest for 20 minutes. Remove twine. Slice pork and transfer to a platter along with onions. Squeeze juice of reserved lemon into skillet and whisk to incorporate. Serve pan juices with the pork and onions.

# Vegetables and Sides

As cooks, we find our deepest inspiration in markets overflowing with beautiful, freshly picked produce. These ingredients are the beginning of meals that fully express a sense of place and season: tender Southern cream peas simmered with smoky bacon, potatoes gratin baked under a blanket of tangy Gruyère, or Thai-style green beans spiced with chiles and fish sauce. Call them side dishes if you like, but we know full well that these vibrant vegetables are good enough to take center stage.

*A market scene in Bangkok, where vendors sell produce as well as freshly prepared foods.*

# Potatoes Gratin

A casserole of creamy potatoes beneath a layer of bubbly Gruyère cheese is known variously as potatoes gratin, *gratin dauphinois*, and scalloped potatoes. Over years of trial and error, SAVEUR executive food editor Todd Coleman developed the recipe for this sumptuous, perfectly browned gratin, an excellent match for baked ham or prime rib.

| | |
|---|---|
| 5 | tbsp. unsalted butter, cubed |
| 2 | cloves garlic, minced |
| | Kosher salt, to taste |
| 6 | large waxy potatoes (about 2½ lbs.), such as red bliss, peeled and cut crosswise into ⅛-inch rounds |
| 2 | cups half-and-half |
| | Freshly ground black pepper, to taste |
| | Freshly grated nutmeg, to taste |
| 1 | cup grated Gruyère cheese |

*Serves 6*

**1.** Heat the oven to 400°F. Grease an 8-inch square baking dish with 1 tbsp. of the butter and set aside. Make a garlic paste by sprinkling the garlic with a little salt and scraping the garlic repeatedly against a work surface with the side of a knife.

**2.** Combine the garlic paste, potatoes, half-and-half, and remaining butter in a 4-qt. saucepan over medium-high heat and bring to a boil. Season with salt, pepper, and nutmeg and cook, stirring occasionally, until the potatoes are just tender and the mixture has thickened, about 10 minutes.

**3.** Transfer the mixture to the prepared baking dish, smoothing the top. Sprinkle the cheese over the gratin and bake until golden brown and bubbly, 30–40 minutes. Let the gratin cool slightly before serving.

**COOKING NOTE** *Potatoes gratin tastes best when the potatoes retain some firmness. Low-starch, or waxy, varieties such as red bliss, French fingerling, and white rose are best suited to the task. So-called "all-purpose" potatoes like Yukon Golds are also lower in starch and will hold up almost as well as waxy potatoes after cooking. Testing a potato's starch level is easy: drop the spud into a pot containing 2¾ cups of water and ¼ cup table salt. If the potato sinks, it's a floury variety (that is, dense with starch); if it floats, it's a waxy variety.*

## The Easy Way

Few things are more satisfying than a crusty gratin, straight out of the oven. Years ago, when I learned to make the dish, I took great pains to shingle layer upon layer of the sliced potatoes carefully into the baking dish before covering them with cream and cheese, repeatedly pressing down on the slices so that they would remain submerged in the liquid while they baked. It was laborious and slow and, I discovered, kind of a waste of time. No careful layering or ovenside tending is needed if you add a simple preliminary step: Combine all the ingredients except the cheese in a pot, cook until the mixture thickens (the potatoes cook partially, releasing some of their starch and absorbing some of the cream), and transfer the mixture to a casserole dish before topping it with cheese and baking it. You still get the same delicious result without any of the fuss. —*Todd Coleman*

# Chiles Rellenos

This central Mexican specialty of deep-fried chiles filled with melted cheese and served with a cinnamon-scented tomato sauce is popular in restaurants and home kitchens on both sides of the U.S.–Mexico border. We love this recipe from La Abeja, a Mexican-American café in Los Angeles, for its airy egg-white batter, which puffs and crisps around the chiles as they fry.

2 lbs. ripe tomatoes, peeled, cored, and roughly chopped

1 tbsp. kosher salt, plus more to taste

½ tsp. ground cinnamon

3 cloves garlic, roughly chopped

5 sprigs fresh cilantro, plus more to garnish

1 small yellow onion, roughly chopped

1 serrano chile, roughly chopped
Freshly ground black pepper, to taste

8 Anaheim or poblano chiles, about 6 inches long
Canola oil, for frying

8 ½ x ½ x 4-inch long strips Monterey Jack cheese

1 cup flour

8 egg whites, plus 1 yolk
Crema or sour cream, to garnish
Crumbled cotija or feta cheese, to garnish

*Serves 8*

**1.** Combine the tomatoes, salt, cinnamon, garlic, cilantro, onions, and serrano chiles in a blender and purée until smooth. Transfer the mixture to a 2-qt. pot and bring to a boil over medium-high heat. Reduce the heat to medium-low and simmer, stirring occasionally, until slightly thickened, about 10–12 minutes. Season the sauce with salt and pepper and set aside to keep warm.

**2.** Using a paring knife, cut about ½ inch from the bottom tip of each Anaheim chile. Using a thin knife, scrape out and discard veins and seeds and set the chiles aside.

**3.** Pour oil to a depth of 2 inches into a 6-qt. Dutch oven and heat over medium-high heat until a deep-fry thermometer reads 350°F. Add the chiles and cook, turning occasionally, until their skin starts to brown and blister, about 2–3 minutes. Using tongs, lift the chiles from the oil to let drain and transfer them to a baking sheet. Let them cool slightly and then peel and discard skins. Remove pan from heat.

**4.** Stuff each chile with 1 strip of Monterey Jack cheese. Place ½ cup flour in a shallow bowl and dredge the chiles in the flour, shaking off the excess, and set aside. Whisk the egg whites in a medium bowl until soft peaks form, then add the remaining flour and egg yolk, and whisk to combine, making a batter.

**5.** Heat oil to 350°F. Working in 2 batches, hold each chile by its stem and dip it into the batter, letting the excess batter drain. Nestle the chile into the frying oil. Cook, turning once, until the chiles are deep golden brown and crisp, 6–8 minutes. Transfer the chiles to a paper towel–lined plate to drain.

**6.** Divide the sauce between serving plates and top each with a fried chile. Garnish with crema, cotija cheese, and cilantro and serve immediately.

①

②

③

④

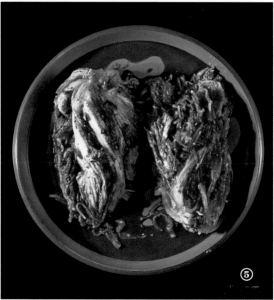

⑤

⑥

⑦

⑧

⑨

# Kimchi Pancakes

Anyone who has tried Korean food knows kimchi, the pungent pickled vegetables used both as a condiment and an ingredient in spicy, soulful dishes like these crisp-fried pancakes, made with *paechu* (cabbage) kimchi and ground pork. The recipe makes about 25 small pancakes, but you can also cook large ones that fill the bottom of the skillet and then slice them into wedges to serve.

| | |
|---|---|
| ¼ | lb. ground pork |
| 2 | cups chopped cabbage kimchi (paechu) |
| 1 | cup flour |
| ½ | cup rice flour |
| 6 | scallions, minced |
| 1 | egg, lightly beaten |
| 10½ | tbsp. canola oil |
| | Kosher salt, to taste |

*Serves 4–6*

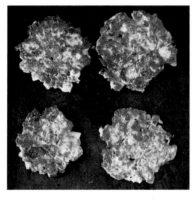

**1.** Combine the ground pork, kimchi, flour, rice flour, scallions, egg, and 1 cup ice-cold water in a bowl; whisk to combine. Set the batter aside to rest for 10 minutes.

**2.** Working in 7 batches, heat 1½ tbsp. oil in a 12-inch nonstick skillet over medium-high heat. Scoop four 2-tbsp. portions of batter into the skillet and flatten each portion with the back of a spoon. Cook until the edges crisp, about 2 minutes. Flip the pancakes and cook until set, about 2 minutes more. Transfer the pancakes to paper towels and wipe out the skillet after each batch. Repeat with the remaining oil and batter. Serve the pancakes sprinkled with salt.

## A World of Kimchi

Though cabbage (*paechu*) kimchi and daikon (*mu*) kimchi are the two best-known versions of the food, literally hundreds of other kinds exist. Pictured on the facing page are nine varieties that hint at the astonishing diversity of flavor, color, and texture that kimchi can possess. ① **Tongchimi kimchi**, or water kimchi, can be any number of fermented pickles that are often served in their brining water; the version shown contains Asian pear, daikon, scallions, pomegranate seeds, and chiles. ② **Uong kimchi** is made with woodsy-tasting, crunchy burdock root and is usually aged for just a day or so. ③ For **muchae kimchi**, crisp daikon radishes are shredded into long strands before being fermented in a thick, pungent paste of chile powder and garlic. ④ The broad leaves of the herb perilla (also known as beefsteak), which have a distinctive cinnamon-like flavor, are the base for **kaennip kimchi**, which has a refreshing bite. ⑤ **Paechu kimchi**—brined cabbage leaves rubbed with a paste of ground chiles, garlic, salted shrimp, anchovy sauce, and scallions and aged in jars—is a staple in Korean households and the most widely available kimchi in Asian markets in the United States. ⑥ **Gat kimchi** is an intensely flavorful pickle of mustard leaves and stems that have been fermented with anchovies and glutinous rice paste. ⑦ The big, pumpkin-like squash called *rumbo* that's harvested in the fall in Korea is frequently used as the base for a sumptuous, mildly sweet dish called **hobak kimchi**. ⑧ A kind of Korean wild lettuce called **kodulpacgi** is the base for this slightly sour kimchi; over time, the firm leaves become soft and pliable. ⑨ **Naeng-myun kimchi** is a striking, peppery pickle of thin-sliced daikon radishes that have usually been aged for only a few days and are often garnished with scallions and sliced chiles.

# Thai-Style Green Beans with Chile and Basil

*Tua Kaek Pad Prik Pao*

The roasted chile paste called *nam prik pao*—a pantry staple in Thailand that can be found in most Asian markets in the United States—lends smoky heat and an earthy, salty-sweet flavor to stir-fried green beans.

3   tbsp. peanut oil
8   cloves garlic, roughly chopped
1   lb. green beans, trimmed and cut into 2-inch lengths
3   tbsp. nam prik pao (Thai roasted chile paste, or any jarred Asian chile paste)
1   tbsp. fish sauce
1   cup torn Thai basil leaves

*Serves 4*

**1.** Heat a 14-inch flat-bottomed wok or a skillet over high heat. Add the oil and swirl to coat the pan. When the oil is hot and almost smoking, add the garlic and cook, stirring constantly, for 10 seconds. Add the green beans and stir-fry for 1 minute.

**2.** Stir in the chile paste, toss to coat the green beans, and cook, stirring occasionally, until the beans are crisp-tender, about 6 minutes. (Sprinkle in a little water if the pan gets too hot and the beans brown too quickly.) Add the fish sauce and basil, toss to combine, and serve.

# Zucchini Fritters

*Kolokitho Keftedes*

On the Greek island of Crete, cooks transform bumper crops of summer vegetables into a wide array of *mezedes*, or small dishes. These parsley-flecked zucchini fritters can be served hot or at room temperature.

| | |
|---|---|
| 1 | lb. zucchini, grated |
| 2 | tsp. kosher salt |
| ½ | cup minced flat-leaf parsley |
| ½ | cup grated Pecorino Romano |
| ½ | cup dried bread crumbs |
| 1 | medium yellow onion, grated |
| 1 | egg, beaten |
| | Freshly ground black pepper, to taste |
| | Pinch of cayenne pepper |
| | Olive oil or canola oil, for frying |

*Serves 4*

**1.** Mix the zucchini and salt in a strainer; set a weighted plate on top and let drain for about 30 minutes. Transfer the zucchini to a tea towel and squeeze out the liquid. Mix together the zucchini, parsley, cheese, bread crumbs, onions, and egg in a bowl. Season with the pepper and cayenne. Divide the mixture into 12 balls and press the balls into ¾-inch thick patties.

**2.** Pour oil into a 4-qt. pot to a depth of 2 inches and heat over medium-high heat until a deep-fry thermometer reads 315°F. Working in 2 batches, fry the patties, turning once, until browned and crisp, 5–6 minutes. Using a slotted spoon, transfer the fritters to paper towels to drain. Serve warm or at room temperature.

## Small Wonders

The small plates known as *mezedes* are essential to the Greek way of eating. Served as snacks or appetizers in homes and tavernas, they make a convivial beginning to a meal. They're also designed to accompany drinks, as it's frowned upon in Greece to drink without food. (As long as you're eating, it's safe to order another round.) Greeks have been eating this way since ancient times; the third-century author Athenaeus, for instance, writes of meals that centered on "a large tray on which are five small plates." *Mezedes* can range from humble to fancy. The simplest—oil-cured olives, feta sprinkled with oregano—are known as *pikilia*, which means "assortment," and they usually arrive free of charge with any order of spirits, wine, or beer. Some *mezedes* are regional (like stuffed mussels, a specialty from Thessaloniki), while others are seasonal (like the fava beans and chickpeas you'll see diners shelling at their tables in spring). Then there are the classics you'll find always and everywhere: grilled octopus; garlicky dips served with bread; the rice-and-herb-filled grape leaves called dolmades; cheese-and-tomato-laden baked dishes called *saganaki*; and the ubiquitous fritters, known as *keftedes*, made with meat or vegetables. By convention, one starts with the cold vegetables, spreads, and pickles, continues on to cold seafood, and finishes with the fried and warm foods. Whoever has "the quickest fork," as the old saying goes, succeeds in tasting them all. —*Aglaia Kremezi*

### Smoky, Hot

You might find peppers stuffed with cheese (pictured at right) in a taverna in Athens or in other parts of Greece, but this classic dish is associated above all with the region of Macedonia, in the north. Peppers—mild and hot, fresh and dried—are one of the agricultural glories of the region, and the queen of them all is the sweet, firm-fleshed, long red pepper grown around the town of Florina, in the mountains of Macedonia's far northwest. I ate these stuffed Florina peppers at Myrovolos Smyrni, an *ouzeri*, or ouzo bar, in business since the 1950s in the Macedonian city of Thessaloniki. (A waitress from Aristotelous, another Thessaloniki *ouzeri,* is pictured on the facing page.) The filling is a whipped feta dip called *htipiti,* which is spiked with hot chiles; some versions get a tangy boost from fresh lemon juice. It's a powerful combination of flavors, but then this is food designed as a match for anise-flavored ouzo or the equally potent spirit *tsipouro. Htipiti* is often served with pita for dipping, but in this case it's stuffed inside the split Florina peppers, which are broiled until they're black around the edges and the *htipiti* is golden and bubbly. The result—salty, sweet, smoky, hot, and luscious all at once— embodies the bold cuisine of the region better than any other dish I know.
—*Beth Kracklauer*

# Peppers Stuffed with Feta
*Piperies Gemistes Me Feta*

Cooks in northern Greece make this *meze,* or small dish, with the sweet, red Florina peppers grown in that part of the country. You can substitute Anaheim chiles, which have a good deal of sweetness, or Fresnos for a little more heat.

| | |
|---|---|
| 10 | 3–4-inch Fresno chiles, or six 4–5-inch Anaheim chiles |
| 9 | oz. feta, crumbled |
| 2 | tbsp. extra-virgin olive oil |
| 2 | tbsp. Greek yogurt |
| 1 | tbsp. minced fresh parsley |
| 1/3 | tsp. lemon zest |
| 1/4 | tsp. dried oregano |
| 2 | egg yolks |
| | Kosher salt and freshly ground black pepper, to taste |
| 1/4 | cup grated Parmigiano-Reggiano |

*Serves 4–6*

**1.** Arrange a rack 6 inches from the broiler element and set oven to broil. Put peppers on a baking sheet and broil, turning once, until just soft, about 5 minutes. Transfer to a rack; let cool.

**2.** In a large bowl, use a hand mixer to whip feta, oil, yogurt, parsley, zest, oregano, and egg yolks; season with salt and pepper. Make a lengthwise cut from the stem to the tip of each pepper; scoop out and discard seeds and ribs. Stuff each pepper with some of the feta filling; transfer peppers to an aluminum foil–lined baking sheet; chill for 30 minutes. Sprinkle peppers with grated cheese; broil peppers until cheese is golden brown and bubbly, about 6 minutes. Transfer peppers to a platter and serve hot.

# Creamy Spiced Indian Lentils

*Dal Makhani*

This velvety Punjabi stew is simmered for hours, until the lentils all but disintegrate and the flavors of cumin, coriander, garam masala, and other spices bloom, deepen, and intermingle. The name, *dal makhani*, is itself a testament to the stew's richness: *Makhan* is the Hindi word for butter, and this dish contains plenty of it.

| | |
|---|---|
| 1½ | cups whole black lentils |
| ½ | cup split yellow lentils |
| ½ | cup small red kidney beans |
| 1 | tbsp. mustard or canola oil |
| 6 | cloves garlic, coarsely chopped |
| 2 | Thai green chiles, stemmed and coarsely chopped |
| 1 | 2-inch piece peeled ginger, coarsely chopped |
| 6 | tbsp. clarified butter |
| 1 | tsp. cumin seeds |
| 1 | medium red onion, chopped |
| 1 | tsp. ground coriander |
| 1 | tsp. ground turmeric |
| 1 | cup canned peeled whole tomatoes, puréed |
| 2 | tbsp. garam masala |
| 1 | tbsp. dried fenugreek leaves, optional |
| 1 | tsp. Kashmiri red chile powder or paprika |
| | Salt, to taste |
| 1½ | cups milk |
| 8 | tbsp. unsalted butter, cut into pieces |
| ½ | cup heavy cream |

*Serves 6–8*

**1.** Combine lentils and kidney beans and wash under running water until it runs clear. Toss with oil in a bowl; set aside. Purée garlic, chiles, ginger, and ¼ cup water in a blender; set paste aside.

**2.** Heat clarified butter in a large pot over medium-high heat. Add cumin; cook for 1 minute. Add onions and cook until browned, 8–10 minutes. Add paste, coriander, and turmeric; cook 3 minutes. Add tomatoes and cook, stirring and scraping until thickened, 6–7 minutes. Add the lentil mixture and 2 quarts water; bring to a boil. Reduce heat to medium-low; simmer, covered, until tender, about 2 hours.

**3.** Add garam masala, fenugreek, chile powder, and salt to taste; simmer for 5 minutes. Stir in milk and butter; simmer for 5 minutes. Drizzle cream on top and serve.

## The Art of the Wok

In Beijing, where I live, I've met cooks from all over China, and they've taught me a lot about their respective regional cuisines. The one common denominator they all share is stir-frying—not a single technique, but a whole approach to cooking that involves quickly preparing dishes over high heat in a wok, with ingredients added in a measured progression so that each one cooks to the point of optimal flavor and texture.

One of the best stir-fry cooks I've ever met is Pan Suefen (pictured at right), a native of Taiwan who lives in Beijing. Suefen is fanatical about sourcing her ingredients, and stir-frying is a technique that brings out their best flavor and texture. For

instance, stir-frying shiitake mushrooms, which she dries herself in her own living room, magnifies their earthy taste and fragrance. For such a delicious ingredient, Suefen insists, no sauce, no aromatics are called for; just heat, oil, salt, and sugar, applied with care. Constant stirring and flipping ensures that every morsel gets equal exposure to the center of the wok, where the heat is the most intense.

The mushrooms are cooked with bok choy, and I love the pleasing transformation the vegetable undergoes in the wok: the crunchy white stem develops a caramelized flavor as it's left alone for a minute with its cut surface in direct contact with the wok, and the leaves wilt slightly, acquiring a mild sweetness as they cook.

What strikes me as I watch Suefen cook is the way that just a few elements—wok, oil, a handful of ingredients—can produce endlessly varied results depending on how a cook chooses to use them. —*Lillian Chou*

# Stir-Fried Mushrooms and Bok Choy

*Donggu Pei Shucai*

This is stir-frying at its purest and best: no sauce to make, no complicated steps to follow, just the judicious exposure of food to heat. Each ingredient remains in the wok long enough to undergo the desired transformation and not a moment longer; the mushrooms' earthy fragrance seems to magnify many times over, while the bok choy takes on a vivid color and a mildly sweet flavor.

| | |
|---|---|
| 6 | large dried mushrooms, such as shiitake |
| 1 | tbsp. canola oil |
| ½ | lb. small Shanghai or baby bok choy, halved lengthwise (about 10 heads) |
| ¼ | tsp. sugar |
| | Kosher salt, to taste |

*Serves 2–4*

**1.** Put mushrooms into a medium bowl of water and soak for 2 hours. Drain and squeeze any excess water from the mushrooms and cut off their stems. Cut mushrooms into ¼-inch thick slices. Heat a 14-inch wok (or skillet) over high heat until wok begins to smoke. Add oil around the edge of the wok and swirl to coat bottom and sides. Add mushrooms and cook, stirring and tossing constantly, until fragrant, about 2 minutes. Transfer mushrooms to a plate and set aside.

**2.** Return wok to high heat until it begins to smoke. Add bok choy cut side down, along with 2 tbsp. water, and cook, without stirring, until the water evaporates, about 1 minute.

**3.** Add sugar and season with salt. Vigorously stir and toss bok choy until it's bright green and wilted, about 1 more minute.

**4.** Return mushrooms to wok, toss to combine, and cook until the flavors meld, about 30 seconds. Transfer mushrooms and bok choy to a serving platter and serve hot or at room temperature.

*Sun Guoying, a home cook in Mutianyu, a village near Beijing, China, stir-fries a dish of eggs and scallions in her kitchen.*

This casserole's roots can be traced to mid-century America, a time and place that gave rise to a number of one-dish meals made with readily available and inexpensive ingredients. The version many of us grew up with was invented by the Campbell Soup Company in 1955 and called for a trinity of convenience foods: canned Durkee or French's fried onions, Green Giant canned green beans, and Campbell's condensed cream of mushroom soup. The recipe had been invented to fulfill a request from Cecily Brownstone, the prominent food editor at the Associated Press, who sought help in reproducing a dish she'd tasted at a press dinner. The dinner took place at the home of John Snively, a wealthy citrus rancher in Florida, and his wife, May. The conceit of the event was that the Snivelys had served a replica of the evening's menu to Iranian royalty: Shah Mohammed Reza Pahlevi and his wife, Queen Soraya (pictured at left), who had recently paid a visit to the ranch. Mrs. Snively had presented a delicious green bean casserole made with cream sauce and mushrooms. The queen, Mrs. Snively told the assembled members of the press, had apparently loved the casserole and "had eaten [it] with gusto." With that, Brownstone had her story and, thanks to some help from the Campbell Soup test kitchen, an easy-to-make recipe. The article she wrote was headlined "Beans Fit for an Iranian Queen," and it sparked a national love affair with the dish. Over the years, the Campbell Soup Company has subtly altered the recipe, but the basics of the iconic dish have remained essentially unchanged.

# Green Bean Casserole

There will always be a place in our hearts for the 1950s-style version of this classic casserole, the one made with canned cream of mushroom soup and store-bought fried onions. Still, using fresh ingredients is nearly as easy, and, it must be said, the results are a whole lot tastier.

| | |
|---|---|
| 3 | cups chicken stock |
| ½ | oz. dried shiitake mushrooms, stemmed |
| | Kosher salt, to taste |
| 2 | lbs. green beans, cut into 2-inch pieces |
| | Canola oil, for frying |
| 1¼ | cups flour |
| 2 | small yellow onions, thinly sliced |
| 5 | tbsp. unsalted butter |
| ⅓ | cup heavy cream |
| | Freshly ground black pepper, to taste |

*Serves 6–8*

**1.** Bring the stock to a boil in a small pot. Remove from the heat and add the dried mushrooms. Cover and let soften for about 20 minutes. Strain and reserve the broth. Thinly slice the mushrooms and set aside. Meanwhile, bring a pot of salted water to a boil. Add the green beans and cook until tender, 6–7 minutes. Chill the beans in an ice bath, drain, and pat dry.

**2.** Pour oil into a large pot to a depth of 2 inches and heat over medium-high heat until a deep-fry thermometer reads 350°F. Put 1 cup flour into a bowl. Working in batches, toss the onions in the flour, shake off the excess, and fry until golden brown, 3–4 minutes. Transfer to a paper towel–lined plate and season with salt.

**3.** Heat the oven to 375°F. Grease an 8-inch square casserole with 1 tbsp. butter and set aside. Melt the remaining butter in a saucepan over medium heat. Whisk in the remaining flour and cook for 1 minute. While whisking, pour in the reserved broth and bring to a boil. Reduce the heat to medium-low and simmer, whisking occasionally, until thickened, 15–20 minutes. Whisk in the cream, remove from the heat, and add the reserved green beans, half the fried onions, the reserved mushrooms, and salt and pepper. Transfer to the prepared casserole, top with the remaining onions, and bake until bubbly, about 20 minutes. Serve warm.

# Butter Risotto

*Risotto alla Milanese*

We usually think of olive oil when we think of Italian cuisine, but home cooks in Italy, particularly in the north, use plenty of butter, too. In Milan, for instance, they make this sumptuous risotto by sautéing rice in butter before simmering it in a saffron-infused stock, and then they stir in even more butter just before serving.

| | |
|---|---|
| 6 | cups chicken stock |
| ⅛ | tsp. saffron threads |
| 9 | tbsp. unsalted butter |
| 1 | small yellow onion, minced |
| 2 | cups vialone or arborio rice |
| 1 | cup grated Grana Padano cheese |

*Serves 4*

**1.** Bring the stock to a bare simmer in a saucepan over medium heat. Put the saffron and ½ cup hot stock into a small bowl, cover, and set aside to let the saffron bloom. Cover the stock and keep warm.

**2.** Heat 5 tbsp. butter in a medium pot over medium heat. Add the onions and cook, stirring, until softened, 2–3 minutes. Add the

rice and cook, stirring constantly with a wooden spoon, until opaque, 4–5 minutes.

**3.** Add ½ cup stock and cook, stirring often, until the stock is mostly absorbed, about 3 minutes. Add another ½ cup stock, stirring often, and repeat the process until all the stock is uscd, about 25 min utes total. Continue cooking the rice until just al dente, about 3 minutes more.

**4.** Set a fine mesh strainer over a bowl; strain the saffron-infused stock and set the saffron threads aside. Pour the saffron-infused stock into the rice and cook, stirring constantly, about 2 minutes. Gently stir in the saffron threads. Remove the pan from the heat and stir in the remaining butter and half of the grated cheese. Serve the risotto with the remaining cheese on the side.

## Brilliant Bulb

When I was growing up, my Italian-American family used fennel every which way. Its dried, anise-scented seeds studded my grandfather's home-made sweet pork sausage, and its fresh, feathery fronds were chopped up and sprinkled into everything from salads to bean soups. At the end of each meal, after the plates were cleared and the coffee was poured, slices of the crisp, raw bulb were brought to the table as a refreshing palate cleanser. When I started travelling to Italy as an adult, I encountered this versatile vegetable in even more preparations that highlighted its sweet flavor. In Sicily, slender wild fennel fronds are chopped and tossed with sardines, pine nuts, and pasta, and in the north, the bulbs are grilled and drizzled with balsamic vinegar, or baked until soft and creamy. —*Dana Bowen*

# Fennel Baked in Cream

*Finocchio al Forno*

Chef Gabrielle Hamilton of Prune restaurant in New York City turned us on to this simple, classic Italian preparation. Baking fennel in the oven with cream and Parmigiano-Reggiano cheese makes for a luxurious gratin with a delectable caramelized top.

| | |
|---|---|
| 1½ | lbs. fennel (about 2 large bulbs), stalks removed, halved lengthwise, and cut into ½-inch wedges |
| 2 | cups heavy cream |
| 1½ | cups finely grated Parmigiano-Reggiano Kosher salt and freshly ground black pepper, to taste |
| 4 | tbsp. unsalted butter, cubed |

*Serves 6–8*

**1.** Heat oven to 425°F. In a bowl, toss together fennel, cream, and 1 cup cheese and season with salt and pepper. Transfer to a 3-qt. baking dish and dot with the butter. Cover dish with foil and bake for 1 hour.

**2.** Uncover the baking dish and sprinkle the top with the remaining cheese. Continue baking until fennel is tender and top is well browned, about 30 minutes. Serve immediately.

# Boone Tavern's Spoonbread

This soft, luxurious spoonbread marks the start of most meals at Kentucky's century-old Boone Tavern (pictured at left). The eggy corn bread pudding rises and settles like a soufflé and goes exceptionally well with that other Kentucky specialty, smoky and salty country ham.

4 tbsp. unsalted butter,
1 tbsp. softened and
3 tbsp. melted
3 cups milk
1¼ cups finely ground
white cornmeal
1 tsp. baking powder
1 tsp. kosher salt
2 eggs, beaten

*Serves 6–8*

**1.** Grease a 9-inch round cake pan with some of the softened butter. Cut out a parchment paper circle to fit inside the pan, nestle it into the bottom, and grease the paper with the remaining softened butter. Set the prepared cake pan aside.

**2.** In a 2-qt. saucepan, bring the milk to a boil, whisking occasionally, over high heat. While whisking, pour in the cornmeal in a steady stream. Whisk vigorously to incorporate the cornmeal, for about 1 minute. Remove the pan from the heat and set aside to let the cornmeal mixture cool to room temperature.

**3.** Heat the oven to 350°F. Transfer the cornmeal mixture to the bowl of a standing mixer fitted with a paddle attachment. Add the melted butter, baking powder, salt, and eggs and mix on medium speed until uniform and aerated, about 15 minutes.

**4.** Pour the cornmeal batter into the prepared pan and bake until golden brown and puffy and a toothpick inserted in the center comes out clean, about 1 hour and 20 minutes. Serve immediately.

## Southern Belle

Off State Highway 78 in central Kentucky you'll find Boone Tavern, a century-old restaurant and hotel. Situated on the campus of Berea College, the establishment earned wide acclaim under Richard T. Hougen, who managed it from 1940 to 1976 and popularized such dishes as Pork Chops the Tricky Way, Chicken Flakes in a Bird's Nest, and Kentucky Chess Pie. But the most popular item at this Southern institution is the spoonbread, a creamy corn bread soufflé (pictured at left

held by a waitress) that's been served before each meal for more than 60 years. And while the building has undergone an overhaul, Bruce Alcorn, a Boone Tavern cook who, along with fellow old-timer Rawleigh Johnson, has been making the custardy pudding for decades, assures us that the spoonbread has not: "Me and Rawleigh made it back then, we make it now; nothing's changed."

## Lovely Legumes

There are dozens of varieties of Southern peas (which mostly fall into the genus *Vigna unguiculata*), but we're especially fond of the five shown here, for their versatility, distinctive appearance, and flavors. The **zipper cream** ①, developed by a Florida agronomist in 1972, gets its name from the fact that the peas can be whisked from their hull in a zipping motion. Though not in the same genus as Southern peas, **butter beans** ② have a similarly luscious texture and taste and are often lumped into the Southern-peas category; we like the speckled variety shown below. The light-hued, unblemished surface of **cream peas** ③ accounts for the name, though the moniker is often attributed to the cooked peas' butter-soft texture. The **pink-eyed purple hull** ④ has a red spot at the center of each pea, and an earthy taste. **Crowders** ⑤ have a squarish shape, a result of their being densely packed inside the hull (hence the name); brown crowders (shown), which have a deep, earthy flavor, are most prevalent in the South. Fresh-frozen Southern peas are available all year in supermarkets across the region, and can also be ordered online through websites like southwesternproduce.com. In the summer, you can find them fresh at Southern farmers' markets.

# Randy Evans's Southern Peas

Randy Evans, the executive chef at Brennan's restaurant in Houston, grew up on slow-cooked Southern peas, also known as field peas or cowpeas. He recommends simmering them along with a ham hock, carrots, celery, and chopped onion and serving them with corn bread to sop up the smoky-sweet liquor that accumulates during cooking.

| | |
|---|---|
| 1 | tbsp. extra-virgin olive oil |
| 1 | small onion, minced |
| 1 | rib celery |
| 1 | small carrot, peeled |
| 2 | cups fresh or frozen Southern peas (such as zipper creams, black-eyeds, or butter beans) |
| 2½ | cups chicken stock |
| 1 | small smoked ham hock Kosher salt and freshly ground black pepper, to taste Corn bread, for serving |

*Serves 4*

**1.** In a 4-qt. saucepan, heat the oil over medium-high heat. Add the onion and cook, stirring occasionally, until soft and translucent, about 10 minutes.

**2.** Cut the celery and carrot in half and add both to the pan along with the peas, stock, and ham hock. Bring to a boil, lower the heat to medium, and simmer, stirring occasionally, until tender and creamy, about 1 hour. (The time depends on the type and size of the peas; cook smaller peas about 50 minutes and larger ones about one hour and 10 minutes.)

**3.** Remove the ham hock, slice the meat from the bone, and chop; return the meat to the pan and discard the bone. Season the peas with salt and pepper and serve with corn bread.

# Baked Goods and Sweets

Everyday ingredients can undergo remarkable transformations. Sugar becomes caramel, butter becomes butterscotch, egg whites become meringue. The metamorphosis from simple to sublime is the product of forceful whisking, patient stirring, and meticulous timing—processes that are as scientific as they are artful. From rustic sweets like huckleberry crisp and sticky buns to more lavish desserts, like a ganache-topped caramel tart, the meal's sweet finish makes us feel like a kid again.

*Dietmar Muthenthaler, the head chef of Demel, the legendary pastry shop in Vienna, Austria.*

# Chive and Cheddar Biscuits

It seems that every Southern cook has a cherished recipe for homemade biscuits, but this one is a standout. Generous amounts of butter and buttermilk impart richness and a tender texture, and the sharp, tangy flavors of fresh chives and cheddar cheese provide a mouthwatering counterpoint.

2 cups flour, plus more
 for dusting
2 tbsp. baking powder
½ tsp. baking soda
1 tbsp. sugar
1½ tsp. kosher salt
8 tbsp. cold unsalted butter,
 cut into thin pats
¾ cup plus 2 tbsp. buttermilk
½ cup shredded sharp
 cheddar cheese
½ cup minced chives
2 tbsp. heavy cream

*Makes 6 biscuits*

**1.** Heat the oven to 450°F. Whisk together the flour, baking powder, baking soda, sugar, and salt in a bowl. Using a pastry cutter, work the cold butter into the flour mixture until the butter is the size of small peas.

**2.** Add the buttermilk, cheddar, and chives to the flour–butter mixture and stir with a fork to form a loose dough.

**3.** Turn the dough out onto a floured surface and gently pat into a 6 x 9-inch rectangle. Fold into thirds as you would a letter and pat into a 6 x 9-inch rectangle again. Dip the edges of a 3-inch round biscuit cutter in flour and punch out 6 biscuits from the dough. Transfer the biscuits to a parchment paper–lined baking sheet. (Form and cut the dough scraps into another biscuit or two, if you wish; they won't rise as high, though.) Brush the tops with heavy cream and bake until lightly browned, 14–16 minutes. Serve warm.

### Belly Pulpit

As big as the plate they're served on and crisp around the edges, the tender buttermilk flapjacks at Robie's Country Store & Deli, in Hooksett, New Hampshire, a town of 13,000 people in the southeastern part of the state, are so incomparably delicious that they nearly outshine the establishment's other claim to fame: politics. The old-fashioned general store, with its eight café tables and its counter lined with jars of penny candy for sale, is a frequent stop for campaigning politicians passing through the state. Campaigners have long made a habit of pulling up a chair at out-of-the-way, all-American spots like Robie's in the hope that their enthusiasm for down-to-earth, local meals would make them more appealing to voters. Robie's is particularly significant because it's one of the earliest and most anticipated stops on the cross-country campaign trail: New Hampshire traditionally holds one of the first primary elections of the voting season, so the nation naturally turns its attention to the state. Robie's also functions as a community social club: Dorothy Robie, who ran the store for five decades with her husband, Lloyd (whose great-grandfather bought the place in 1887), can still be found having coffee and flapjacks with neighbors there a few times each week.

# Buttermilk Flapjacks

The ideal flapjack is browned and crisp around the edges and tender and fluffy inside. According to the seasoned cooks at Robie's Country Store & Deli, in Hooksett, New Hampshire, for the best results, you've got to take your time and cook the flapjacks one by one with plenty of butter in a hot skillet.

| | |
|---|---|
| 2 | cups flour |
| 2 | tbsp. granulated sugar |
| 4 | tsp. baking powder |
| 1 | tsp. baking soda |
| 1 | tsp. fine sea salt |
| 12 | tbsp. unsalted butter, plus more for serving |
| 2 | cups buttermilk |
| 1 | tsp. vanilla extract |
| 2 | eggs, lightly beaten |
| | Maple syrup, for serving |
| | Confectioners' sugar, for serving |

*Serves 2–4*

**1.** Put the flour, granulated sugar, baking powder, baking soda, and salt into a large bowl and whisk to combine; set aside.

**2.** Melt 4 tbsp. butter. Whisk together the melted butter, buttermilk, vanilla, and eggs in a medium bowl. Pour the buttermilk mixture into the flour mixture and whisk together until just combined to make a thick batter. (For tender flapjacks, don't overmix the batter.)

**3.** Heat an 8-inch nonstick skillet over medium heat. Add 1 tbsp. butter and heat until the butter's foam subsides. Ladle in about ½ cup of the batter. Cook the flapjack, turning once, until deep golden brown on both sides, about 5 minutes total. Transfer to a large ovenproof serving platter and keep warm in a low oven. Repeat the process with additional butter and remaining batter to make 8 flapjacks in all. Serve hot, topped with butter and maple syrup and a dusting of confectioners' sugar.

# Huckleberry Crisps

August is the height of the wild huckleberry season in the Pacific Northwest, where the tiny purple, intensely sweet fruit is harvested from mountain meadows and used in pies, milk shakes, tarts, crisps, and even in savory dishes. These individual-size desserts, with their crumbly brown sugar topping, can be made with fresh or frozen huckleberries or with the fruit's close cousin, blueberries.

| | |
|---|---|
| 6 | tbsp. plus ½ cup granulated sugar |
| 6 | tbsp. flour |
| ¼ | cup rolled oats |
| ¼ | cup packed light brown sugar |
| ¼ | cup chopped walnuts |
| 1 | tsp. lemon zest plus 2 tsp. fresh lemon juice |
| ¾ | tsp. vanilla extract |
| ½ | tsp. kosher salt |
| ¼ | tsp. ground cinnamon |
| 4 | tbsp. unsalted butter, softened |
| 2 | tsp. brandy |
| 4 | cups huckleberries or blueberries |
| 2 | tbsp. cornstarch |
| | Crème fraîche or vanilla ice cream, for serving |

*Serves 4*

**1.** Heat oven to 350°F. Place four 6-oz. ceramic ramekins on a parchment paper–lined baking sheet.

**2.** In a medium bowl, combine 6 tbsp. granulated sugar, flour, oats, brown sugar, walnuts, lemon zest, ¼ tsp. vanilla, ¼ tsp. salt, and cinnamon. Using your fingers, work the butter into the flour mixture until crumbly; transfer the topping to the freezer to chill for 30 minutes.

**3.** In a large bowl, stir together the remaining granulated sugar, salt, and vanilla, along with the lemon juice, brandy, huckleberries, and cornstarch. Divide the berry mixture between the ramekins. Mound some of the topping over each ramekin and bake until the berries are bubbly and the topping is browned, 35–40 minutes. Top each crisp with a dollop of crème fraîche or ice cream and serve.

## A World of Butter

Butter is integral to baked goods and sweets: whether we're creaming it into cake batter, rubbing it into biscuit dough, melting it over pancakes, or blending it with brown sugar to make a streusel topping, it works its rich magic in myriad ways. Various styles have emerged around the world, each one reflecting different regional tastes and production methods. **Cultured butter** ① is made from cream in which fermentation—the conversion of milk sugars into lactic acid—has begun to take place. Most butters are made from pasteurized cream, a process that kills naturally occurring bacteria, so, for this style, lactic-acid bacteria are added to induce fermentation and create a sharper, "cultured" taste that many European bakers prefer. **Salted butter** ② can come in both cultured and uncultured versions. Salted butters make for an emphatically flavored condiment or spread. Pungent-tasting preserved butters such as **smen** ③, a Moroccan delicacy, belong to a variety known as fermented butter; they have been allowed to age for anywhere from two weeks to two years. Among the most prized butters in this country are **raw-cream butters** ④, which are made from unpasteurized farm-fresh cream, an ingredient that's hard to get your hands on if you don't live on or near a dairy farm. Butter that's been heated so that its water content evaporates and has had its milk solids removed is referred to as **clarified butter** ⑤. This pure, long-lasting butterfat, popular in India (where it is called *ghee*), has a high smoke point and is ideal for frying, as well as baking; it is also mixed with nuts and chickpea flour to make fudge-like sweets called *barfi*. Uncultured butter made from fresh, pasteurized cream is generally referred to as **sweet cream butter** ⑥ and is the most common choice for baking. Americans' predilection for chilled yet spreadable butter led to the development of **whipped butter** ⑦, which has nitrogen gas whipped into it after it has been churned, so that it will remain soft at low temperatures. It's wonderful spread on a bagel, but is a poor choice for cooking.

# Sopaipillas

The puffy, deep-fried dough squares known as sopaipillas in New Mexico are just one of a number of delicious fried breads found on both sides of the United States–Mexico border. Often dusted with sugar or drizzled with honey, they are a cousin of Mexican *buñuelos* and American Indian fry bread and are best eaten seconds after coming out of the frying oil, when they're at their lightest and crispest. Pictured at right is Gabriela Bojalil, a home cook in Puebla, Mexico, who gave us this recipe.

2¼   cups flour
1½   tsp. sugar
  1   tsp. baking powder
  1   tsp. kosher salt
  ¼   cup milk, at room
       temperature
1½   tsp. canola oil, plus
       more for frying
  ¼   cup sugar mixed with
       1 tsp. ground cinnamon,
       for serving
  1   cup honey, for serving

*Serves 8–12*

**1.** In a large bowl, whisk together the flour, sugar, baking powder, and salt; add the milk, vegetable oil, and ½ cup of lukewarm water and stir until a sticky dough forms. Transfer the dough to a lightly floured work surface and knead until soft and no longer sticky, about 2 minutes. Cover the dough with a damp cloth and let it rest for 15 minutes. Divide the dough into 3 equal pieces, form each into a ball, and cover again; let rest for 30 minutes.

**2.** Pour canola oil into a 6-qt. Dutch oven to a depth of 2 inches and heat over medium-high heat until a deep-fry thermometer reads 370°F.

**3.** Working with one dough ball at a time, roll out the dough on a lightly floured surface into an 8-inch square. Cut the square into 4 equal smaller squares, and repeat with the remaining dough balls to create 12 squares total.

**4.** Place 4 squares in the oil and fry, turning once, until they're golden brown on both sides, about 2 minutes. Using a slotted spoon, transfer the sopaipillas to paper towels to drain. Repeat with the remaining dough squares. While hot, sprinkle the sopaipillas with cinnamon-sugar, drizzle with honey, and serve.

# Key Lime Pie

This Key lime pie is based on the one served at Joe's Stone Crab, a Miami restaurant. You can use tiny, intensely flavorful Key limes or bottled Key lime juice, though ordinary Persian lime juice works well, too.

| | |
|---|---|
| 1 | cup plus 2½ tbsp. graham cracker crumbs |
| ⅓ | cup sugar |
| 5 | tbsp. unsalted butter, melted |
| 1½ | tbsp. lime zest (from 2 limes) |
| 3 | egg yolks |
| 1 | 14-oz. can sweetened condensed milk |
| ⅔ | cup fresh lime juice, preferably from Key limes |
| 1 | cup heavy cream, chilled |
| 1 | tbsp. confectioners' sugar |

*Serves 8*

**1.** Heat oven to 350°F. Pulse cracker crumbs, sugar, and butter in a food processor to combine. Press evenly into bottom and sides of a 9-inch pie pan. Bake until lightly browned, about 10 minutes. Let cool.

**2.** In a medium bowl, beat lime zest and egg yolks with a hand mixer until pale and thick, about 5 minutes. Add milk and beat until thickened, 3–4 minutes more. Add lime juice; mix until smooth. Pour filling into pie crust; bake until filling is just set in the middle, 8–10 minutes. Let the pie cool.

**3.** In a medium bowl, whisk cream and confectioners' sugar to stiff peaks. Spread whipped cream over the top of pie and chill 2–3 hours before serving.

## Sour Power

Tangy, creamy Key lime pie derives its tartness from its tiny but powerful namesake fruit, the Key lime. Native to Asia and grown now in tropical and subtropical regions worldwide, the Key lime, a Ping-Pong ball–size citrus fruit also known as the West Indian or Mexican lime, is the most widely used lime in kitchens outside the United States. It's an essential ingredient in everything from salads to noodle dishes to marinades, prized for its dynamic acidity (which is at its greatest when the fruit is green and unripe) and copious juice. Mixed with eggs and sweetened condensed milk, the Key lime's zest and juice make for an intensely citrusy pie filling. The flavor of the Persian lime, the cultivar most readily available in U.S. markets, is much milder by comparison. So, why aren't Key limes as widely used here as in the rest of the world? It has to do with the fruit's checkered new-world history. Arriving in the Caribbean with Christopher Columbus, the Key lime thrived in the United States up through the early twentieth century. Then, in 1926, a hurricane wiped out most of Florida's crop, which was replaced with plantings of the larger, thicker-skinned Persian lime, considered sturdier and therefore easier to cultivate and transport. A few of the original trees survived in the Florida Keys, where the fruit acquired its American name and where, in the nineteenth century, the eponymous pie was invented.

# Snickerdoodles

These sweet, spicy cookies are a classic example of how beautifully the flavor of cinnamon blooms in butter.

| | |
|---|---|
| 3 | cups flour |
| 2 | tsp. cream of tartar |
| 1 | tsp. baking soda |
| ¼ | tsp. kosher salt |
| 1¾ | cups sugar |
| 16 | tbsp. unsalted butter, at room temperature |
| 5 | tsp. ground cinnamon |
| 1½ | tsp. vanilla extract |
| 2 | eggs |

*Makes 48 cookies*

**1.** In a medium bowl, whisk together flour, cream of tartar, baking soda, and salt; set aside. Using a handheld mixer on medium speed, beat 1½ cups sugar and the butter together in a medium bowl until pale and fluffy, 2 minutes. Add 2 tsp. cinnamon and the vanilla; beat for 1 minute more.

**2.** Add eggs one at a time, beating well after each addition. Add reserved dry ingredients; mix on low speed until just combined. Refrigerate dough for 30 minutes.

**3.** Heat oven to 375°F. Combine remaining sugar and cinnamon in a small bowl. Remove dough from refrigerator and, using a 1-tbsp. measure, spoon out 48 portions, rolling each portion into a 1-inch ball as you go. Roll each ball in the cinnamon–sugar mixture to coat. Arrange dough balls 2 inches apart on 2 parchment paper–lined baking sheets. Bake until golden brown, about 10 minutes. Transfer to a rack and let cool. Store in an airtight container for up to 3 days.

# Dulce de Leche Cake

*Pastel de Cuatro Leches*

The Spanish name for this dessert, popular in the Dominican Republic, is *pastel de cuatro leches*—"four-milks cake"—a nod to its four key components: heavy cream, sweetened condensed milk, evaporated milk, and the milk-based caramel sauce *dulce de leche*. That last ingredient is, literally, the frosting on the cake and also what sets it apart from the more common *pastel de tres leches*.

| | |
|---|---|
| 2 | tsp. unsalted butter |
| 1 | tbsp. plus 2 cups flour |
| 2 | tsp. baking powder |
| 1½ | tsp. fine sea salt |
| 6 | eggs, at room temperature, separated |
| 1¼ | cups sugar |
| ½ | cup whole milk |
| 1½ | tbsp. dark rum |
| 1 | tbsp. vanilla extract |
| 1 | 14-oz. can sweetened condensed milk |
| 1 | 12-oz. can evaporated milk |
| 1 | cup heavy cream |
| 1 | 16-oz. jar dulce de leche (milk caramel) |

*Serves 8–10*

**1.** Heat the oven to 350°F. Lightly grease a 9 x 13-inch baking pan with the butter and dust with 1 tbsp. of the flour. Invert the pan, tap out the excess flour, and set aside.

**2.** Sift together the remaining flour, baking powder, and salt into a bowl and set aside. Put the egg whites into a large bowl and beat with a hand mixer on medium speed until soft peaks form, about 2 minutes. While the mixer is still running, add the sugar in a gradual stream and continue beating again to medium peaks. Add the egg yolks 1 at a time, beating well after each addition. Alternately add the reserved flour mixture and the whole milk in 3 parts, beating until smooth after each addition. Add the rum and vanilla and beat again briefly until smooth.

**3.** Pour the cake batter into the reserved baking pan and bake until golden brown, 25–30 minutes. Set the cake aside and let cool slightly for 30 minutes.

**4.** Whisk together the sweetened condensed milk, evaporated milk, and heavy cream in a bowl. Using a knife, poke the cake with holes all over, penetrating to the bottom of the pan. Pour the milk mixture over the warm cake and set aside to cool completely.

**5.** Cover the cake with plastic wrap and refrigerate until well chilled and the liquid is absorbed, at least 4 hours. Spread the dulce de leche across the top of the cake and serve.

# Chocolate–Caramel Tart

In this tart—served at the Brooklyn, New York, restaurant Marlow & Sons and its sister restaurant, Diner (server Lindsay Debach is pictured at right)—a layer of chocolate ganache sprinkled with coarse sea salt gives way to a center of gooey caramel. Dutch-process cocoa powder, less bitter than other cocoa powders, is the best choice for the crumbly, cookielike crust.

**FOR THE CRUST:**

1½ cups flour

¼ cup plus 1 tbsp. Dutch-process unsweetened cocoa powder

¼ tsp. kosher salt

10 tbsp. unsalted butter, cubed and softened

½ cup plus 2 tbsp. confectioners' sugar

2 egg yolks, at room temperature

½ tsp. vanilla extract

**FOR THE CARAMEL:**

1½ cups granulated sugar

3 tbsp. light corn syrup

¼ tsp. kosher salt

6 tbsp. unsalted butter

6 tbsp. heavy cream

1 tbsp. crème fraîche

**FOR THE GANACHE:**

½ cup heavy cream

4 oz. bittersweet chocolate, finely chopped

Gray sea salt, for garnish

*Serves 8–10*

**1.** Make the crust: Heat the oven to 350°F. Combine the flour, cocoa powder, and salt in a medium bowl and set aside. Using a handheld mixer, cream together the butter and confectioners' sugar in a large bowl until the mixture is pale and fluffy. Mix in the egg yolks and vanilla and then mix in the reserved dry ingredients. Transfer the dough to a 9-inch fluted tart pan with a removable bottom and press the dough evenly into the bottom and up the sides of the pan. Refrigerate for about 30 minutes.

Prick the tart shell all over with a fork and bake until cooked through, about 20 minutes. Transfer to a rack and let cool.

**2.** Make the caramel: In a 1-qt. saucepan, whisk together the granulated sugar, corn syrup, salt, and 6 tbsp. water and bring to a boil over medium-high heat. Cook, without stirring, until caramel smells toasted and takes on a deep amber color (and a candy thermometer inserted into the syrup reads 365°F). Remove the pan from the heat and whisk in the butter, cream, and crème fraîche (the mixture will bubble up) until smooth. Pour the caramel into the cooled tart shell and let cool slightly; refrigerate until firm, 4–5 hours.

**3.** Make the ganache: Bring the cream to a boil in a 1-qt. saucepan over medium heat. Put the chocolate into a medium heat-proof bowl and pour the hot cream over the chocolate; let sit for 1 minute, then stir slowly with a rubber spatula until smooth.

**4.** Pour the ganache evenly over the tart and refrigerate until set, 4–5 hours. Sprinkle the tart with the sea salt, slice, and serve chilled.

# Katharine Hepburn's Brownies

A version of this recipe accompanied an interview with the actress Katharine Hepburn in the August 1975 issue of *The Ladies' Home Journal*. This brownie recipe, which calls for a smaller than average amount of flour, produces incredibly chewy bars with a full but mellow chocolate flavor.

| | |
|---|---|
| 8 | tbsp. unsalted butter, plus more for greasing |
| 2 | oz. unsweetened chocolate |
| 1 | cup sugar |
| 2 | eggs, beaten |
| ½ | tsp. vanilla extract |
| 1 | cup roughly chopped walnuts |
| ¼ | cup flour |
| ¼ | tsp. fine salt |

*Makes 9 brownies*

**1.** Heat the oven to 325°F. Grease an 8 x 8-inch baking pan with butter. Line pan with parchment paper; grease the paper. Set the pan aside.

**2.** Melt the butter and the chocolate together in a 2-quart saucepan over low heat, stirring constantly with a wooden spoon. Remove the pan from heat and stir in the sugar. Add the eggs and vanilla and stir to make a smooth batter. Add the walnuts, flour, and salt; stir until incorporated. Pour the batter into the baking pan and spread evenly. Bake until a toothpick inserted into the center comes out clean, 40–45 minutes. Let cool on a rack. Cut and serve.

# Red Velvet Cake

According to one legend, red velvet cake was invented in the 1950s at Oscar's restaurant, in New York's Waldorf-Astoria hotel. Another tale—passed on by Raven Dennis of Brooklyn's Cake Man Raven Confectionary, who also shared this recipe with us—traces the cake's origins to the Civil War–era South.

**FOR THE CAKE:**

| | |
|---|---|
| 3 | cups plus 2 tbsp. cake flour; more for dusting pans |
| 1½ | cups sugar |
| 1 | tsp. baking soda |
| 1 | tsp. cocoa powder |
| 1 | tsp. salt |
| 2 | eggs |
| 1½ | cups vegetable oil |
| 1 | cup buttermilk |
| 2 | tbsp. (1 oz.) red food coloring |
| 1 | tsp. vanilla extract |
| 1 | tsp. white distilled vinegar |
| | Butter, for greasing pans |

**FOR THE FROSTING:**

| | |
|---|---|
| 12 | oz. cream cheese, softened |
| 12 | oz. butter, softened |
| 1½ | tsp. pure vanilla extract |
| 3 | cups confectioners' sugar |
| 1½ | cups chopped pecans |

*Makes one 8-inch cake*

**1.** Make the cake: Preheat the oven to 350°F. Sift together cake flour, sugar, baking soda, cocoa, and salt into a medium bowl. Beat eggs, oil, buttermilk, food coloring, vanilla, and vinegar in a large bowl with an electric mixer until well combined. Add dry ingredients and beat until smooth, about 2 minutes. Divide batter evenly between 3 greased and floured 8-inch round cake pans. Bake cakes, rotating pans halfway through, until a toothpick inserted in the center of each cake comes out clean, 25–30 minutes. Let cakes cool 5 minutes, invert each onto a plate, then invert again onto a cooling rack. Let cakes cool completely before frosting.

**2.** Make the frosting: Beat cream cheese, butter, and vanilla together in a large bowl with an electric mixer until combined. Add sugar and beat until frosting is light and fluffy, 5–7 minutes.

**3.** Put 1 cake layer on a cake plate; spread one-quarter of the frosting on top. Set another layer on top and repeat with frosting. Set remaining layer on top, and frost top and sides with the remaining frosting. Press pecans into the sides of the cake. Chill for 2 hours to set frosting, if you like.

# Ice Cream with Butterscotch Sauce

Cooking butter with sugar causes its milk solids to caramelize and take on deep, toasty flavors as well as a gorgeous saffron color. What you end up with is butterscotch. The soda jerks at Franklin Fountain, in Philadelphia (pictured at left), serve it on cherry-topped sundaes and other old-fashioned confections, but butterscotch works equally well when simply drizzled over a couple of scoops of good vanilla ice cream.

| | |
|---|---|
| 8 | tbsp. unsalted butter |
| 2 | tbsp. light corn syrup |
| ¾ | cup granulated sugar |
| ¼ | cup light brown sugar |
| ⅓ | cup heavy cream |
| 1 | tsp. dark rum |
| 1 | tsp. vanilla extract |
| ½ | tsp. fine sea salt |
| ½ | tsp. fresh lemon juice |
| | Vanilla ice cream, for serving |

*Makes 2 cups*

**1.** Heat the butter, corn syrup, and ¼ cup water in a medium saucepan over medium-low heat, stirring constantly, until the butter has melted.

**2.** Stir in the granulated sugar and brown sugar, scraping down the sides of the pan with a rubber spatula. Bring the mixture to a boil over medium heat, without stirring. Cook until the sauce is light brown and a candy thermometer inserted in the sauce reads 245°F, 6–8 minutes.

**3.** Remove the saucepan from the heat. Carefully add the cream, rum, vanilla, salt, and lemon juice and stir to combine. Let the sauce cool to room temperature. Serve drizzled over scoops of vanilla ice cream.

**COOKING NOTE** *To make a butterscotch swirl ice cream, spread softened vanilla ice cream in a baking pan. Top it with ⅓ cup or more of butterscotch sauce (cooled, not hot), and swirl the sauce through the ice cream using a rubber spatula. Return the ice cream to the freezer until the ice cream sets, then serve.*

*The Lilly Lunch Bunch—retired employees of the Eli Lilly pharmaceutical company—having vanilla ice cream sundaes with their choice of toppings at the Hollyhock Hill Restaurant in Indianapolis, Indiana.*

# Lindy's Cheesecake

This cheesecake, a favorite at the Manhattan delicatessen Lindy's, can be put together almost entirely in the food processor, which means it's not only easy to make but also remarkably smooth and light in texture. The shortbread crust tastes of butter, lemon, and vanilla scraped straight from the bean; the airy filling is flecked with lemon and orange zest; and a blast in a very hot oven gives the top a golden color.

**FOR THE CRUST:**

| | |
|---|---|
| 2 | cups flour |
| ¼ | cup sugar |
| 1 | tsp. lemon zest |
| ¼ | tsp. salt |
| 1 | vanilla bean, halved lengthwise, seeds scraped and reserved |
| 8 | tbsp. unsalted butter, cut into ¼-inch cubes |
| 2 | tbsp. vegetable oil |
| 1 | egg yolk |

**FOR THE FILLING:**

| | |
|---|---|
| 2½ | lbs. cream cheese, softened |
| 1¼ | cups sugar |
| 3 | tbsp. flour |
| 1½ | tsp. lemon zest |
| 1½ | tsp. orange zest |
| ½ | tsp. pure vanilla extract |
| 5 | eggs plus 2 egg yolks |
| ¼ | cup heavy cream |

*Makes one 9-inch cake*

**1.** Make the crust: Heat the oven to 400°F. Combine flour, sugar, lemon zest, salt, and vanilla seeds in a food processor and pulse until evenly incorporated. Add butter and pulse until pea-size crumbles form, about 10 pulses. Add oil and egg yolk and pulse until a dough forms. Press dough into the bottom and halfway up the side of a 9-inch spring-form pan; refrigerate for about 30 minutes. Bake until golden brown at the edges and set, 15 minutes; transfer to a wire rack and let cool.

**2.** Make the filling: Preheat oven to 500°F. Combine cream cheese, sugar, flour, zests, and vanilla in a food processor and process until very smooth, about 1 minute.

Add eggs and yolks one at a time, processing 10 seconds after each addition, until smooth; stir in cream. Pour filling into crust (filling will come over the crust), set on a baking sheet, and bake until top is deep golden brown, about 10 minutes. Reduce heat to 200°F and bake for 1 hour more. Transfer to a wire rack and let cool completely to room temperature. Wrap in plastic wrap and refrigerate overnight.

**3.** Remove cake from pan and let sit at room temperature for 1 hour to soften slightly. Cut cake into slices and serve.

## New York Icon

The story of New York cheesecake, like that of so many beloved American foods, is a narrative of immigrant tradition, disputed pedigree, and local pride. The city's signature dessert owes its existence in large part to Philadelphia cream cheese, which was invented in Chester, New York, in 1872 and distributed by a company called Philadelphia Brand. Jewish immigrants from Eastern Europe made do with the cheese when they couldn't find fresh-curd varieties like cottage and farmers' for their traditional baked goods. How this Americanized cheesecake was introduced into New York City mythology has long been a subject of debate. Arnold Reuben, of the Manhattan delicatessen that bears his name, claimed he was the first to serve it, around 1910. Reuben's main competitor, deli man Leo Lindemann, lured away Reuben's Swiss-born pastry chef, Paul Heghi, to re-create the dessert at his establishment, Lindy's, where it became a New York icon.

# Caramel Coconut Flan

Many traditional recipes for this custardy Mexican sweet call for cooking it on the stove top, but baking it is easier and results in an equally sumptuous texture and flavor. A rich combination of coconut milk, evaporated milk, and sweetened condensed milk makes for an especially silky flan.

1 cup sweetened condensed milk
¾ cup evaporated milk
½ cup unsweetened coconut milk
¾ tsp. vanilla extract
¼ tsp. kosher salt
3 eggs plus 3 egg yolks
1½ cups sugar

*Serves 8*

**1.** Arrange a rack in the middle of the oven and heat the oven to 325°F. Heat the condensed milk, evaporated milk, and coconut milk in a 1-qt. saucepan over medium heat until it just begins to simmer; remove from the heat. In a large bowl, whisk together the vanilla, salt, eggs, and yolks until smooth. Whisking constantly, slowly drizzle in the warm milk mixture until incorporated; set aside.

**2.** Stir together the sugar and ½ cup water in a 2-qt. saucepan over medium-high heat. Cook, without stirring, until the sugar turns a deep caramel color, about 15 minutes. Remove the pan from the heat and pour equal amounts of the caramel mixture into eight 6-oz. ramekins; let cool.

**3.** Put 4 ramekins each into two 8-inch square glass baking dishes and pour an equal amount of the reserved milk mixture into each ramekin. Pull out the oven rack and place the baking dishes on it, side by side. Pour enough boiling water into the baking dishes that it comes halfway up the sides of the ramekins. Bake until the custard is just set but still wiggly in the center, about 30 minutes. Covering your hand with a kitchen towel or an oven mitt, pick up the ramekins, transfer them to the refrigerator, and let chill for about 3 hours.

**4.** To serve, use a knife to cut around the inside edges of each ramekin and immerse the bottom of each ramekin in a baking pan of hot water for 20 seconds; invert the ramekins onto small plates to release the flans.

# German Chocolate Cake

Don't let the name fool you: This cake is a slice of pure Americana. The first known recipe, which appeared in a Dallas, Texas, newspaper in the 1950s, called for German's Sweet Chocolate, a popular home-baking ingredient. This version is crowned with the traditional coconut–pecan frosting and leaves the sides bare for a just-right balance of deep cocoa flavor and luscious, nutty topping.

**FOR THE FROSTING:**

| | |
|---|---|
| 1½ | cups sugar |
| 1¾ | cups unsalted butter, softened |
| 1½ | tsp. vanilla extract |
| 4 | egg yolks |
| 1 | 12-oz. can evaporated milk |
| 1½ | cups roughly chopped pecans |
| 7 | oz. package sweetened shredded coconut |

**FOR THE CAKE:**

| | |
|---|---|
| 1 | cup unsalted butter, softened, plus additional butter for greasing the pans |
| 4 | oz. German's Sweet Chocolate, chopped |
| 2 | oz. unsweetened chocolate, chopped |
| 2 | cups flour |
| 1 | tsp. baking soda |
| ¼ | tsp. kosher salt |
| 1½ | cups sugar |
| 4 | egg yolks |
| 1 | tsp. vanilla extract |
| 1 | cup buttermilk |
| 4 | egg whites |

*Serves 12–14*

**1.** Make the frosting: Combine the sugar, butter, vanilla, egg yolks, and evaporated milk in a 2-qt. pot over medium heat. Bring to a simmer and cook until thick, about 12 minutes. Strain through a sieve into a bowl and stir in the pecans and coconut. Chill the frosting in the refrigerator until firm.

**2.** Meanwhile, make the cakes: Heat the oven to 350°F. Grease three 9-inch round cake pans with butter and line the bottoms with parchment circles. Grease the parchment and set aside. Put the chocolates into a small heat-proof bowl, pour in ½ cup boiling water, and let sit for 1 minute. Stir until smooth, then set aside. In another bowl, whisk together the flour, baking soda, and salt and set aside.

**3.** In a standing mixer, beat together 1¼ cups sugar and the butter until fluffy. Add the egg yolks, one at a time. Add the melted chocolate mixture and the vanilla and beat until smooth. On a low speed, alternately add the flour mixture and buttermilk until just combined; set the batter aside.

**4.** Whip the egg whites to soft peaks. Add the remaining sugar and whip to stiff peaks. Fold the egg whites into the batter; divide between the pans and smooth the batter. Bake until the cakes are set, 25–30 minutes. Transfer the cakes to racks and let cool in the pans for about 5 minutes, then run a knife around the sides of the cakes and invert them onto a rack to cool to room temperature.

**5.** Place 1 layer on a cake stand or a platter and spread one-third of the frosting over the top, leaving the sides bare. Repeat with the next 2 layers to assemble the cake. Slice into wedges and serve.

# Drinks

A good drink revives and refreshes us, warming or cooling us from the inside out. The best drinks—a glass of milky-sweet *masala chai*, fragrant with cardamom; a spicy bloody mary spiked with vodka and horseradish; a rich black-and-white malted milk shake—complement the foods on the table, but they are just as wonderful when sipped on their own.

*A group of friends drink* masala chai *at a dhaba, or truck stop, in Delhi, India.*

# Spiced Tea

*Masala Chai*

A far cry from the so-called *chai* drinks sold at chain coffee shops in the United States, this sweet, milky tea gets its invigorating piney fragrance from the crushed pods of green cardamom.

| | |
|---|---|
| ½ | cup evaporated milk |
| 5 | tsp. sugar |
| 6 | black tea bags |
| 5 | pods green cardamom, crushed |

*Makes 4½ cups*

Bring milk, sugar, tea, cardamom, and 4 cups water to a boil in a 2-qt. saucepan. Remove from heat and let steep for 5 minutes. Strain and serve hot.

## Precious Pods

Of the two main varieties of cardamom, green cardamom (*Elettaria cardamomum*) is the one that's more common. Its floral perfume penetrates all sorts of invigorating beverages, both hot and cold, from Indian *masala chai* and frothy yogurt *lassis* to potent Turkish coffee; many gins are flavored with it, too, and some bartenders keep a bottle of simple syrup infused with cardamom on hand for mixing into cocktails. It brightens chicken curries throughout South Asia and dozens of Scandinavian sweets and pastries, like *pulla*, a braided challah-like loaf, and *semlor*, Finnish cream puffs filled with rich cardamom-scented pastry cream. Green cardamom pods are small and oval, containing tiny black seeds that are crushed or ground to release their sweet, eucalyptus-like fragrance. Its cousin, black cardamom (*Amomum subulatum*), which grows in much larger, brown pods, is smoky and bold from drying over wood fires. It's perfect for infusing earthy depth into a Pakistani lamb *biriyani* or other roasted meats as well as full-flavored stews. Both spices are grown primarily in India; Guatemala, Costa Rica, Tanzania, and Sri Lanka, too, grow significant quantities of the green variety, while black cardamom also comes from the Himalayan regions of Nepal, China, and Bhutan. For the best flavor, buy the spices whole and grind them yourself in a spice grinder or with a mortar and pestle.

## Precious Powder

We love milk shakes of all sorts, but we're especially ardent devotees of the malted version. Malteds get their toasty, rich flavor from malted milk powder, a combination of malted barley, wheat flour, and whole milk, mixed together and evaporated to a fine dust. There are several brands to choose from, including Carnation and Kitchen Krafts, but we've always preferred Horlick's malted milk powder, which has a wonderfully rounded, mildly sweet taste. The late founders of the company that makes it, James and William Horlick, also happened to be the inventors of the ingredient itself, which they conceived of as a digestive aid and fortifying food for babies. They patented their invention in 1883 in Racine, Wisconsin, where their company was based. In 1890, James brought the company to the brothers' native England. Over there, Horlick's powder mixed with hot milk became a popular bedtime treat. Stateside, however, the malted milk powder went on to inspire the early-twentieth-century milk shake craze. It's often cited that a soda jerk named Ivar "Pop" Coulson invented the malted milk shake at a Walgreens store in Chicago in 1922 when he blended together scoops of vanilla ice cream with Horlick's milk powder and chocolate syrup to create a chocolate shake called "Horlick's Milk Shake." Prior to that, malted milk drinks were made by mixing milk, chocolate syrup, and malted powder in a glass. Coulson's invention went on to become Walgreens' signature shake, and it has inspired countless variations around the world.

# Black-and-White Banana Malted Milk Shake

We adapted this recipe from one in *Thoroughly Modern Milkshakes*, by Adam Ried. Unlike the classic black-and-white, in which chocolate syrup and vanilla ice cream are blended together, this shake has alternating layers of vanilla and chocolate ice cream, with ripe banana and malted milk powder mixed in to add body and rounded sweetness.

| | |
|---|---|
| ½ | cup cold milk |
| 1 | tbsp. malted milk powder, such as Horlick's |
| 1¼ | tsp. vanilla extract |
| ½ | ripe medium banana |
| 1 | pint vanilla ice cream |
| 1 | pint chocolate ice cream |

*Serves 2*

**1.** Place ¼ cup milk, malted milk powder, 1 tsp. vanilla, and banana in a blender and blend until smooth. Add vanilla ice cream and blend, pausing once or twice to mash the mixture with a rubber spatula, until smooth, about 45 seconds. Pour mixture into a pitcher and set aside in the refrigerator.

**2.** Place remaining milk and vanilla extract along with the chocolate ice cream in the blender and blend, pausing once or twice to mash the mixture with a rubber spatula, until smooth, about 45 seconds.

**3.** Layer vanilla and chocolate shake mixtures in 2 large chilled milk shake glasses, beginning and ending with vanilla. Serve immediately with straws.

# Puka Punch

This sophisticated rum cocktail with its dark, spicy depths comes from the Tiki-Ti, a Los Angeles institution and a shrine to well-made tropical drinks. Puka Punch is a relic of the golden age of tiki cocktails, roughly from the 1930s to the 1950s, when some of the most talented mixologists were focusing on exotic drinks. This recipe calls for three different rums, but you can substitute either dark or white rum for any of them.

| | |
|---|---|
| 2 | oz. white rum |
| 1 | oz. fresh lime juice |
| ¾ | oz. dark Jamaican rum |
| ¾ | oz. fresh orange juice |
| ¾ | oz. pineapple juice |
| ¾ | oz. passion fruit syrup |
| 2 | tsp. honey mixed with 2 tsp. hot water and chilled |
| ¼ | oz. falernum (optional) |
| 1 | dash Angostura bitters |
| ¾ | oz. 151-proof rum (optional) Pineapple slice, orange wedge, and maraschino cherry, for garnish |

*Makes 1 cocktail*

**1.** Put 1½ cups ice cubes into a blender and crush. Add first 9 ingredients and blend on high speed. Pour into a tall glass.

**2.** Slowly pour 151-proof rum over back of a spoon into cocktail. Garnish with pineapple, orange, and cherry.

## Polynesian Spirits

They don't serve beer. They don't serve wine. For weeks at a time, they don't serve anything at all—whenever they feel like getting sand between their toes, they close up shop. The owners of the Tiki-Ti in the L.A. neighborhood of Los Feliz are textbook examples of how not to succeed in the bar business; nevertheless, for over 49 years the Buhen family has been slinging Singapore Slings and Missionary's Downfalls for a fanatical following. My first visit was in 1979. I'd previously dismissed tropical cocktails as slushy umbrella drinks, but the Tiki-Ti's came with an impressive pedigree: many of them were invented at the country's first tiki bar, Don the Beachcomber (opened in the mid-1930s), where Ray Buhen, a native of the Philippines, was one of the original bartenders. The Beachcomber attracted a Hollywood crowd and kick-started the midcentury Polynesian craze. Ray Buhen spent the golden age of tiki honing his craft behind some 60 different bars. In 1961, Ray; his wife, Geraldine; and son Michael (pictured at left) opened a place of their own. Ray died in 1999, but his spirit lives on at the Tiki-Ti. —*Jeff Berry*

## Liquid Gold

Rum has always had a good-time reputation in the United States. Midcentury tiki lounges popularized the sugar-cane distillate in whimsical cocktails served in scorpion bowls, ceramic coconuts, and hollowed-out pineapples. Even so, rum is a spirit worth taking seriously. Aged varieties can be savored straight, offering a palette of citrus, vanilla, butterscotch, caramel, and stone fruit. Some of the finest examples are produced on the French Caribbean island of Martinique, the only source of rum with its own *Appellation d'Origine Contrôlée*, the certification created by the French government for quality agricultural products. The parameters for *rhum agricole* are steadfast: it must be made from sugar-cane juice; have a relatively low proof; and when aged, it must be stored for three to 15 years in charred-oak barrels (like the ones pictured below). Until the nineteenth century, sugarcane planters in Martinique distilled rum from molasses, a byproduct of sugar production. But when competition from sugar beets depressed demand for sugarcane, planters discovered that a distillate could be made from pure cane juice at a lower proof than molasses-based rum's, allowing the pleasing flavors of the cane to shine through. Capitalizing on this new method, 150 distilleries flourished on Martinique in the nineteenth century. Today, only eight survive, but producers like Clément and Neissen make some of the finest rums in the world. —*Wayne Curtis*

# Hot Buttered Rum

This drink is a holdover from the colonial period in America, when the harsh edges of old-style rums were softened with the addition of warm butter, dark sugar, and spices. Made with the mellower aged rums available today, it is a smooth, rich, and soothing potion.

| | |
|---|---|
| 1½ | cups (3 sticks) unsalted butter, softened |
| 1 | cup packed dark brown sugar |
| ¼ | tsp. freshly grated nutmeg |
| ¼ | tsp. ground cinnamon |
| ¼ | tsp. ground cloves |
| | Kosher salt, to taste |
| 3 | cups aged rum |

*Serves 16*

**1.** In a large bowl, beat together butter and sugar with a hand mixer set on medium speed until smooth, 1–2 minutes. Add nutmeg, cinnamon, cloves, and a pinch of salt and beat again to combine. Cover bowl with plastic wrap and chill mixture until ready to use.

**2.** To make 1 hot buttered rum, place 2 heaping tbsp. of the chilled butter mixture in an 8-oz. mug along with 1½ oz. rum and fill with boiling water. Stir to melt and mix ingredients; serve immediately.

# Spiced Wine

*Glühwein*

Warming cinnamon thoroughly suffuses this mulled wine; the German name for it, in fact, translates literally as "glow wine." Especially popular at Christmastime, *glühwein* is plenty potent on its own, though aficionados have been known to ask for it *mit schuss*, spiked with a shot of rum. Pictured at left, a Christmas eve dinner in the Berlin home of Werner Blanck, at which generous portions of *glühwein* were consumed.

| | |
|---|---|
| 1 | 750-ml bottle medium-bodied red wine, such as zweigelt |
| ½ | cup sugar |
| 8 | whole cloves |
| 4 | lemon wedges |
| 4 | 4-inch sticks cinnamon |

*Serves 4*

Bring ingredients to a boil, stirring occasionally, in a 4-qt. saucepan and remove from heat. Discard cloves. Ladle wine into 4 glasses and garnish each with 1 of the cinnamon sticks and 1 lemon wedge. Serve hot.

**COOKING NOTE** *Mulling is a method of flavoring liquid by heating it with herbs, spices, and other aromatics. Using whole cinnamon sticks, rather than powder, leads to a gentler extraction of the oils, and a softer flavor. Other whole spices, such as cardamom, nutmeg, and mace, will work just as well in this recipe.*

## Holiday Cheer

In northern Europe, mulled wine announces the arrival of the Christmas season. Vendors at winter markets that pop up throughout the region sell steaming mugs of it, while home cooks brew bubbling pots bound for the holiday table. In fact, though, the festive drink—typically a blend of red wine, citrus fruit, spices, and sugar—predates Christmas by thousands of years. Early civilizations, as far back as 5000 B.C., used heated, spiced wines for many purposes, ranging from the gastronomic to the religious. Romans drank a version called *hippocras*, named for the Greek doctor Hippocrates, because it was believed to have healing properties. The expansion of the spice trade between Europe and the East in the seventeenth century made the flavors we associate with the drink—such as cinnamon, nutmeg, cloves, and mace—more readily available, and today, many countries have their own recipe for mulled wine. In Sweden, *glögg* is scented with cardamom and sometimes fortified with hard liquor; the British make *wassail*, fragrant with ginger, nutmeg, and other spices. In Germany, it's *glühwein*, a comforting concoction heady with cinnamon and holiday cheer.

Muddling sugar and citrus peel is a technique called for in many classic punch recipes. First, use a vegetable peeler to remove the peel of a lemon or an orange in ¾-inch-wide strips, taking care to avoid the bitter white pith. Next, add the strips to a small, heavy bowl along with the amount of sugar specified in the recipe. Finally, use a muddler—the small, baseball bat–shaped stick used by bartenders—or a pestle or wooden spoon

to vigorously crush the sugar and citrus peel together. The abrasive sugar helps rupture the citrus's cell walls and release the flavorful oils within. You'll know that's happened when the sugar takes on the color of the peels and becomes moist, slushy in texture, and intensely fragrant. The result is a concentrated, aromatic base that cuts the astringency of the alcohol in the punch and lends a bright, pleasing taste.

# Regent's Punch

In London in the early part of the nineteenth century, punch houses were upscale gathering places where the fashionable could relax, and punch itself was a dry, complex drink presented with a fair amount of pomp. This one gracefully combines green tea and champagne with various liquors and three kinds of citrus.

| | |
|---|---|
| 1 | cup sugar |
| 1 | cup cubed pineapple |
| 2 | lemons |
| 2 | oranges |
| 1 | Seville orange (also called bitter or sour orange) |
| 2 | green tea bags (or 2 tsp. green tea leaves) |
| 1 | cup brandy, preferably VSOP cognac |
| ¼ | cup dark Jamaican rum |
| ¼ | cup arrack liquor, preferably Batavia-Arrack van Oosten, or cachaça |
| 2 | 750-ml bottles brut champagne, chilled Freshly grated nutmeg |

*Makes 3 quarts*

**1.** In a 1-qt. saucepan, combine ½ cup sugar and ¼ cup water. Stir over high heat until sugar dissolves and transfer to a bowl along with pineapple. Allow to macerate in refrigerator for at least 8 hours to make a pineapple syrup. Strain and reserve; discard solids.

**2.** Using a peeler, peel lemons, oranges, and Seville orange, taking off as little white pith as possible. Transfer peels to a heavy bowl; reserve fruit. Add remaining sugar; use a muddler or a wooden spoon to vigorously crush sugar and peels together until sugar turns faintly yellow and slushy.

**3.** In a medium bowl, steep tea in 2 cups of boiling water for 5 minutes. Strain tea over lemon and sugar mixture; stir until sugar dissolves. Juice reserved fruit into tea mixture. Strain through a sieve into another bowl and discard solids. Stir in pineapple syrup, brandy, rum, and arrack. Chill mixture.

**4.** To serve, combine mixture and champagne in a punch bowl along with a large block of ice. Garnish with nutmeg.

**COOKING NOTE** *Arrack, a fiery sugarcane-based spirit distilled on the Indonesian island of Java—and not to be confused with the grape-based, anise-flavored Middle Eastern spirit called arak—is an essential ingredient in many classic punch recipes. For years it was unavailable in this country, but a new brand, Batavia-Arrack van Oosten, has recently gone on the market. If your liquor store doesn't carry it, Brazilian cachaça will supply some of the arrack's characteristic fire.*

# Six Texan Cocktails

We've always loved the spicy, stick-to-your-ribs cuisine of Texas, but it wasn't until we devoted an entire issue to Texan foodways in the summer of 2009 that we came to understand the Lone Star State's equally impressive way with drinks. There's the elegant yet potent sangria (our favorite is a midcentury recipe from the ladies at the Junior League of Houston), the refreshing cucumber cooler (a signature drink at the bar of the Gage Hotel, in Marathon, Texas), and the still-popular Tex-Mex originals like the garnet-colored Chico (a cocktail born in cantinas along the Texas–Mexico border during World War II). Revitalizing savory cocktails like the tart-spicy beer-based Michelada (all the rage in Austin) and the longhorn bull shot (a nod to the state's cattle industry) will knock the dust off your spurs. And, of course, there are the best margaritas on earth. At right, a few of our favorites.

## Michelada

This peppery and refreshing beer cocktail, a particular favorite in Austin, Texas, is also popular throughout Mexico.

| | |
|---|---|
| 1 | lime wedge |
| | Kosher salt, to taste |
| 1 | oz. fresh lime juice |
| ½ | tsp. Worcestershire |
| ⅛ | tsp. freshly ground black pepper |
| 5 | dashes Tabasco |
| 1 | 12-oz. bottle or can of Mexican beer, such as Tecate or Pacifico |

*Makes 1 drink*

Rub a lime wedge around the rim of a pint glass and dip the rim in salt. Add lime juice, Worcestershire, pepper, and Tabasco. Fill the glass with ice and beer.

## Kentucky Club Margarita

Most historians agree that the Kentucky Club, just across the border from El Paso in Juarez, Mexico, is the birthplace of the margarita. Unlike its sugary frozen cousin, this elegant shaken margarita is more tart than sweet.

| | |
|---|---|
| 1 | lime wedge |
| | Kosher salt, to taste |
| 1½ | oz. silver tequila |
| ¾ | oz. freshly squeezed lime juice |
| ½ | oz. Cointreau |

*Makes 1 cocktail*

**1.** Rub a lime wedge around the rim of a chilled margarita glass and dip the rim in salt to coat.

**2.** In a cocktail shaker, combine tequila, lime juice, Cointreau, and 1 cup crushed ice. Cover and shake vigorously to chill. Strain the drink into the glass.

## Book Club Sangria

Red wine and ginger ale make a tasty base for this fruit-filled punch, popular among members of the Junior League of Houston in the 1970s.

| | |
|---|---|
| ¾ | cup sugar |
| 1 | 750-ml bottle fruity red wine, such as pinot noir |
| ¼ | cup brandy |
| ¼ | cup fresh lemon juice |
| ¼ | cup fresh lime juice |
| ¼ | cup fresh orange juice |
| 1 | cup ginger ale |
| 1 | cup fresh pineapple chunks |
| 4 | thin slices each of orange, lemon, and lime |
| 1 | fresh peach, pitted and sliced |

*Serves 6–8*

Bring sugar and 1 cup water to a boil in a 1-qt. saucepan. Let cool and transfer to a pitcher; add wine, brandy, and citrus juices. Chill. Before serving, add ginger ale, pineapple, citrus slices, and peaches. Stir and serve over ice.

# Longhorn Bull Shot

This is the Texan cattleman's answer to the bloody mary, with beef broth in place of tomato juice and plenty of Tabasco.

- 6 oz. beef broth
- 1½ oz. vodka
- 1 tbsp. fresh lime juice
  Worcestershire, to taste
  Tabasco, to taste

*Makes 1 cocktail*

Combine the broth, vodka, lime juice, Worcestershire, and Tabasco along with a few ice cubes in a tumbler. Stir to combine.

# Cucumber Cooler

The bartenders at the Gage Hotel in Marathon, Texas, make this fresh-tasting cocktail with cucumber and thyme from the kitchen garden and Texas-made Tito's vodka.

- 1 2-inch piece cucumber, thinly sliced crosswise, plus 1 additional slice for garnish
- ⅛ tsp. fresh thyme leaves
- 1½ oz. vodka
- ½ oz. simple syrup

*Makes 1 cocktail*

**1.** In a cocktail shaker, combine the cucumber slices, thyme, and ¼ cup crushed ice.

**2.** Using a muddler, crush ingredients until slushy. Add more ice, vodka, and simple syrup. Cover, shake vigorously to combine, and pour contents into a glass garnished with a slice of cucumber.

# Chico

The Chico, an old cantina favorite, gets its ruby color and earthy sweetness from blackberry liqueur.

- 2 oz. gin or silver tequila
- 2 oz. blackberry liqueur
- 1 oz. simple syrup
- ½ oz. fresh lemon juice
  Club soda, to taste

*Makes 1 cocktail*

Fill a highball glass with ice. Add the gin, liqueur, simple syrup, and lemon juice. Top the drink off with club soda. Gently stir to combine.

Some say the classic eye-opener known as the bloody mary was created by a bartender in Paris in 1921; others claim that same barkeep invented it at the St. Regis Hotel in Manhattan. And then there are those who believe a comedian who promoted the Smirnoff vodka company in the 1950s deserves the credit. No matter who dreamed up the combination of tomato and lemon juices, vodka, Worcestershire sauce, and pepper, the bloody mary has since become America's favorite cocktail. The zesty concoction belongs to a group of drinks called snappers, which are defined by a savory base (like tomato juice) and the condiments that give them their character. The real beauty of a bloody mary—aside from the taste—is its versatility. There are variations all over America that speak to regional tastes and creative whims. Add a freshly shucked East Coast oyster, and the drink tastes of New England. Throw in some pickled okra, and it takes on a Southern accent. On these pages: a tried-and-true recipe for a classic bloody mary, and a few of our favorite riffs on the drink.

# Six Regional Bloody Marys

### Original Bloody Mary

This classic version has been the signature cocktail at the King Cole Bar at New York City's St. Regis Hotel since 1934.

| | |
|---|---|
| 1 | oz. vodka |
| 2 | oz. tomato juice |
| 2 | tsp. fresh lemon juice |
| | Worcestershire, to taste |
| | Kosher salt and freshly ground black pepper, to taste |
| | Cayenne pepper, to taste |
| | Lemon wedge, for garnish |

*Makes 1 cocktail*

Combine ingredients in a mixing glass, stir, and pour into an ice-filled Collins glass. Garnish with lemon.

### Michelada Bloody Mary

SAVEUR contributing editor Rick Bayless suggested this variation, inspired by the Mexican beer cocktail *michelada* (see page 246).

| | |
|---|---|
| 1 | cup tomato juice |
| 1 | oz. fresh orange juice |
| 1 | oz. fresh grapefruit juice |
| 1 | oz. fresh lime juice, plus 1 lime wedge |
| ½ | oz. pomegranate juice (optional) |
| | Kosher salt, for garnish |
| 4 | oz. tequila blanco |
| 1 | 12-oz. bottle Mexican beer |
| | Tabasco, to taste |
| | Worcestershire, to taste |
| 4 | pickled jalapeños, for garnish |

*Makes 4 cocktails*

Combine juices in a pitcher; set aside. Spread salt on a plate. Rub the rim of 4 beer mugs with a lime wedge. Dip rims of mugs into salt. Fill mugs with ice and divide juice mixture between mugs. Add 1 oz. tequila and 3 oz. beer to each. Season with Tabasco and Worcestershire, stir, and add a jalapeño to each glass.

### Cajun Bloody Mary

Pickled okra, beef broth, and a spoonful of tangy mustard make this substantial bloody mary, based on one served at the New Orleans restaurant Cochon, practically a course in itself.

| | |
|---|---|
| 4 | oz. tomato juice |
| 1 | oz. beef broth |
| 1 | tsp. whole-grain mustard |
| 1 | tsp. fresh lemon juice |
| 1 | tsp. fresh lime juice |
| 1 | tsp. red wine vinegar |
| ⅛ | tsp. garlic powder |
| | Tabasco, to taste |
| | Pickled okra juice, to taste |
| | Freshly ground black pepper, to taste |
| 1½ | oz. vodka |
| | Pickled okra, pickled green beans, and caper berries, for garnish |

*Makes 1 cocktail*

In a mixing glass, combine the tomato juice, broth, mustard, lemon juice, lime juice, vinegar, and garlic powder and season with Tabasco, okra juice, and black pepper; refrigerate mixture until chilled. To serve, fill a rocks glass with ice cubes, pour in vodka, and stir in tomato juice mixture. Garnish with okra, beans, and caper berries.

# Old Bay Bloody Mary

Old Bay seasoning gives this drink, served at the Old Ebbitt Grill in Washington, D.C., a savory kick that works well with a garnish of boiled shrimp.

2 tbsp. Old Bay seasoning
1 lime wedge
1½ oz. vodka, preferably pepper flavored
1 oz. beef broth
3 oz. tomato juice
1¼ oz. fresh lemon juice
¼ tsp. freshly ground black pepper
1 large tail-on shrimp, peeled, boiled, and chilled

*Makes 1 cocktail*

Sprinkle Old Bay on a plate. Rub the rim of a small glass with the lime wedge and dip rim in Old Bay to coat. Add cracked ice to glass; set aside. In a mixing glass, combine vodka, beef broth, tomato juice, lemon juice, and black pepper; stir to combine. Pour into reserved glass; garnish with shrimp.

# Heirloom Tomato Bloody Mary

At the Union Square Cafe in New York City, bartenders make this bloody mary using heirloom tomatoes from the nearby farmers' market.

2 large ripe heirloom tomatoes
2 oz. vodka
1 oz. fresh lime juice
1 tsp. freshly grated horseradish
Tabasco, to taste
Sea salt and coarsely ground black pepper, to taste
Cherry or grape tomatoes, for garnish

*Makes 1 cocktail*

Push tomatoes through a potato ricer or a medium sieve into a small bowl; discard solids. Refrigerate juice until chilled. Stir in vodka, lime juice, horseradish, and Tabasco and season with salt and pepper. Fill a highball glass with ice and add tomato juice mixture. Garnish with a wooden skewer threaded with tomatoes.

# Boston Bloody Mary

The raw oysters in this bloody mary, based on one at the Boston restaurant Eastern Standard, impart a hint of brine.

4 oz. tomato juice
2 tsp. fresh lemon juice
⅛ tsp. celery salt
Prepared horseradish, to taste
Worcestershire, to taste
Tabasco, to taste
Kosher salt and freshly ground black pepper, to taste
2 oz. vodka
2 freshly shucked oysters with their juice
2 green olives, for garnish
Celery stalk, for garnish

*Makes 1 cocktail*

In a mixing glass, combine tomato juice, lemon juice, and celery salt and season with horseradish, Worcestershire, Tabasco, salt, and pepper; chill. Fill an old-fashioned glass with ice. Pour in the chilled tomato juice mixture and the vodka. Add oysters and their juice; stir. Garnish with olives and celery.

# Index

# Table of Equivalents

The exact equivalents in the following tables have been rounded for convenience.

## Liquid and Dry Measurements

| U.S. | METRIC |
|---|---|
| ¼ teaspoon | 1.25 milliliters |
| ½ teaspoon | 2.5 milliliters |
| 1 teaspoon | 5 milliliters |
| 1 tablespoon (3 teaspoons) | 15 milliliters |
| 1 fluid ounce | 30 milliliters |
| ¼ cup | 65 milliliters |
| ⅓ cup | 80 milliliters |
| 1 cup | 235 milliliters |
| 1 pint (2 cups) | 480 milliliters |
| 1 quart (4 cups, 32 fluid ounces) | 950 milliliters |
| 1 gallon (4 quarts) | 3.8 liters |
| 1 ounce (by weight) | 28 grams |
| 1 pound | 454 grams |
| 2.2 pounds | 1 kilogram |

## Length Measures

| U.S. | METRIC |
|---|---|
| ⅛ inch | 3 millimeters |
| ¼ inch | 6 millimeters |
| ½ inch | 12 millimeters |
| 1 inch | 2.5 centimeters |

## Oven Temperatures

| FAHRENHEIT | CELSIUS | GAS |
|---|---|---|
| 250° | 120° | ½ |
| 275° | 140° | 1 |
| 300° | 150° | 2 |
| 325° | 160° | 3 |
| 350° | 180° | 4 |
| 375° | 190° | 5 |
| 400° | 200° | 6 |
| 425° | 220° | 7 |
| 450° | 230° | 8 |
| 475° | 240° | 9 |
| 500° | 260° | 10 |

# Acknowledgments

Though I'm listed as the editor of this book, that's only partly true. The fact is I was just one of many collaborators who joined in the journey that led to its making. Foremost among those collaborators are Todd Coleman, executive food editor (and star photographer) at SAVEUR, whose expertise and intelligence grace every page; executive editor Dana Bowen, whose second-to-none editorial instincts set the tone for the entire book; David Weaver, our art director (and book designer), who proved as always to be a model not only of talent but of endless level-headedness; deputy editor, Beth Kracklauer, who patiently wrote (and then re-wrote, many times) the recipe headnotes; managing editors Greg Ferro and Georgia Freedman, who pushed us all to the finish line with (fabulously) cheap jokes, endless optimism, and the occasional jolt-of-fear e-mail; Hunter Lewis, SAVEUR's kitchen director, who along with Ben Mims, assistant kitchen director, diligently tested, multiple times, all the recipes that appear in the book; senior editors Betsy Andrews and Gabriella Gershenson, whose eleventh-hour comments and guidance were invaluable; our scary-smart copy chief Dorothy Irwin and her second-in-command, Kathryn Kuchenbrod; associate editor, Karen Shimizu, assistant editor, Marne Setton, and former SAVEUR deputy editor David McAninch, all of whom provided crucial editorial assistance along the way; and Larry Nighswander, SAVEUR's photo director, who along with Paul Love, Mary Rose Lorenzana, Lyndsey Atkinson, and Katherine Pease culled and gathered the images that appear herein. Additionally, I'm indebted to our production manager, Courtney Janka, and prepress guru, Don Hill and his indefatigable team at Bonnier's headquarters in Winter Park, Florida. My hat goes off to every one of these people not only for their selfless dedication but for their wisdom. Working with them all is a daily source of inspiration.

I'm grateful to the SAVEUR contributors whose writing appears in these pages, including Jeff Berry, Jeffrey Charles, Jay Cheshes, Lillian Chou, Lizzie Collingham, Wayne Curtis, Cathy Danh, Cara de Silva, Sarah DiGregorio, Beth Elon, Evan Kleiman, Aglaia Kremezi, George Motz, Joan Nathan, Alia Yunis, and Robb Walsh. I also want to give a special shout out to our regular stable of photographers who created the images in this book, including André Baranowski, Virginie Blachere, David Brabyn, Bruce Crippen, Penny De Los Santos, Ben Fink, Natalie Fobes, David Hagerman, Michael Kraus, Ariana Lindquist, Landon Nordeman, and Barbara Ries. The brilliant work they do is its true heart and soul.

I also want to thank the ever-cheery and intensely skilled folks at Weldon Owen in San Francisco, whose vision it was to create this book, including Terry Newell, Hannah Rahill, Kim Laidlaw, Amy Kaneko, and Kara Church. Equally crucial to its existence is the terrific team at Chronicle Books, especially Bill LeBlond. Finally, I owe special thanks to Merri Lee Kingsly, publisher of SAVEUR (and one of its fiercest advocates); Terry Snow, CEO of Bonnier Corporation, our parent company; and Jonas Bonnier, chairman of the corporation. You keep us on our toes, you push us toward excellence. —*James Oseland, Editor-in-Chief*

# Photography Credits

**André Baranowski** 12, 16, 18, 19, 27, 44, 50, 53, 58, 59, 62, 65, 77, 78, 82, 86, 87, 91, 94, 100, 102, 107, 108, 110, 118, 125, 129, 130, 134, 135, 137, 140, 150, 151, 160, 163, 164, 175, 189, 191, 196, 197, 200, 203, 204, 206, 213, 214, 216, 223, 226, 230, 237, 243; **Virginie Blachere** 22; **David Brabyn** 40; **Todd Coleman** 14, 20, 21, 25, 28, 31, 32, 35, 42, 47, 48, 55, 57, 70, 74, 81, 96, 97, 104, 121, 145, 149, 152, 167, 170, 171, 173, 174, 177, 178, 179, 180, 181, 185, 186, 192, 193, 208, 210, 211, 218, 221, 227, 229, 234, 235; **Bruce Crippen** 92; **Penny De Los Santos** 9, 10, 24, 38, 39, 66, 67, 69, 88, 89, 114, 122, 141, 154, 156, 157, 182, 183, 209, 232; **Ben Fink** 242; **David Hagerman** 168; **Michael Kraus** 52, 153, 155, 158, 159, 246, 274, 248, 249; **Ariana Lindquist** 119, 238; **Jen Munkvold,** 80; **Larry Nighswander** 60; **Landon Nordeman** 2, 34, 36, 37, 45, 72, 84, 85, 101, 113, 116, 131, 138, 143, 198, 217, 222, 240, 241, 244, 245; **James Oseland** 23, 54, 68, 95, 124, 126, 128, 133, 136, 194, 195, 224; **Barbara Reis** 144, 146; **Corbis:** Owen Franken, 17; Bettmann, 49; Martin Harvey, 98; The Mariners' Museum, 103; A. H. Wilcox, 190; **Getty:** Ralph Crane, 76; **Alamy:** Mirrorpix, 188

Library of Congress Cataloging-in-Publication
data is available.

ISBN: 978-0-8118-7801-2
Manufactured in Singapore

Design by Dave Weaver

Conceived and produced with SAVEUR by
Weldon Owen Inc.
415 Jackson Street, Suite 200, San Francisco, CA 94111
Telephone: 415 291 0100 Fax: 415 291 8841

Weldon Owen wishes to thank the following people for their
support in producing this book: Emma Boys, Lesley Bruynesteyn,
Kara Church, Anna Grace, Brenda Koplin, Kim Laidlaw, David McAnich,
Julia Nelson, Elizabeth Parson, Hannah Rahill

10 9 8 7 6 5 4 3 2 1

Chronicle Books LLC
680 Second Street
San Francisco, CA 94107

www.chroniclebooks.com